SCIENTIFIC METHOD FOR AUDITING

Publications of the
Bureau of Business and Economic Research
University of California

SCIENTIFIC METHOD
FOR AUDITING

Applications of Statistical Sampling
Theory to Auditing Procedure

BY

LAWRENCE L. VANCE

UNIVERSITY OF CALIFORNIA PRESS
BERKELEY AND LOS ANGELES
1950

UNIVERSITY OF CALIFORNIA PRESS
BERKELEY AND LOS ANGELES
CALIFORNIA

◇

CAMBRIDGE UNIVERSITY PRESS
LONDON, ENGLAND

TO

M. L. V. AND A. C. V.

Preface

THE OBJECT *of this work is to make available to the accounting profession some of the techniques developed by statisticians for the interpretation of samples. These techniques have been applied with extraordinary success in recent years to the control of quality of manufactured product, and they have been increasingly exploited as fundamental tools of research in all the sciences. It is of interest that the modern development of statistical theory, which may be identified with the work of Karl Pearson in the early 1890's, began to emerge at the same time that modern auditing practice made its literary debut with the publication, in 1892, of L. R. Dicksee's* Auditing.

Almost all auditing work, particularly in the United States, is done on a sampling basis, but no one has bridged the gap between the sister professions of public accounting and statistics to enable auditors to use rigorous statistical reasoning, although the two professions had a parallel development. The present work attempts to serve this need as far as fundamental, readily available statistical concepts are concerned. Its method is to describe the use of probability inferences based upon the binomial distribution; to present sequential sampling as a basis for the general interpretation of auditing samples; to examine the conditions which auditing imposes upon statistical reasoning; to suggest specific procedures which will give auditing the benefit of objective statistical devices in the selection and interpretation of auditing samples or tests; to discuss their application; and to illuminate the bases thus provided for the establishment of objective, workable auditing standards.

The author desires to express his indebtedness to Professors Ernest A. Heilman and Bruce D. Mudgett of the University of Minnesota for encouragement and painstaking criticism which were given in the initiation and throughout the period of substantial com-

pletion of this work. He is deeply indebted also to Mr. Leonard F. Avery for his assistance in the preparation of the case material and for the contribution of one of the cases; to his colleagues, Professors J. S. Bain, W. L. Crum, L. A. Doyle, R. W. Jastram, and F. L. Kidner of the University of California, and to Messrs. Lewis Lilly and D. J. W. Patrick of McLaren, Goode & Co., Certified Public Accountants, for careful readings and criticism of the manuscript; and to the Bureau of Business and Economic Research of the University of California for its very helpful clerical and financial assistance.

LAWRENCE L. VANCE

Berkeley, 1949

Contents

TABLES

CHAPTER I

Fundamental Concepts

THAT AUDITORS generally base their conclusions on samples or tests of the accounting entries is well known within the profession, though often misunderstood by laymen. Authoritative statements recognizing this situation are numerous. For example, in its statement on *Extensions of Auditing Procedure* of May 9, 1939, the committee on auditing procedure of the American Institute of Accountants refers to the technique as follows: "The committee desires to state its opinion that auditing procedure has kept, and continues to keep, pace with the growth and development of industry and that the well-established custom of making test-checks of accounting records and related data and, beyond that, reliance upon the system of internal check and control after investigation of its adequacy and effectiveness, has with very few exceptions proved sufficient for its purpose." In setting up the procedure of direct confirmation of receivables by correspondence with customers as "normal audit procedure" in the same publication, the committee recommends, in part: ". . . that the method, extent, and time of obtaining such confirmations in each engagement, and whether of all receivables or a part thereof, be determined by the independent certified public accountant as in other phases of procedure requiring the exercise of his judgment."

NEED FOR STATISTICAL THEORY IN AUDITING

Although many standards of auditing procedure are generally recognized, as reference to appendix iii will disclose, they depend to a high degree upon the subjective judgment of the individual auditor for their application. The essential condition in each examination of accounts is that the auditor in charge be satisfied as to the adequacy of the accounting, but the means by which he accepts one sample of transactions as indicating adequate accounting and rejects another—the landmarks by which he recognizes his arrival into the state of satisfaction—are for the most part peculiarly his own. Obviously, there may be differences in the circumstances which lead accountants to accept or reject the conclusion of adequacy in any set of accounts. These arise from what might be termed irrelevant influences: differences in the individual accountant's concepts, or variations in the mood of the individual and in the pressures which weigh upon him at any moment, the most important of which may be the efforts of the client to economize in the cost of auditing. It is not suggested here that the adoption of statistical methods of inference will relieve accountants of the necessity for making subjective judgments; but it should become clear that these methods will enable judgments to be made objectively over more substantial areas of the accounts, and that, in auditing as elsewhere, concepts of statistical theory illuminate the whole process of reaching conclusions from samples. The advantages of objective, statistical judgments are the auditor's freedom from the irrelevant influences referred to above, the greater exactitude with which he can plan his work in any engagement, the possibility of a closer agreement with the client about the amount and cost of work to be done, and the assurance that auditing standards can be made more specific and effective.

Specific questions of the kind every auditor faces daily will illustrate these points. First, let us assume that an auditor has tested the physical count of an inventory of 1,200 items by following the crew of the client and counting 90 of the items himself. He finds that the count of 3 of these 90 items contains significant errors. What shall he conclude as to the accuracy of the count of the remaining 1,110 items? Is it probably accurate enough so that he can certify the balance sheet? Should he perhaps take more samples? Aside from the fact that the nature of the errors discovered will have a bearing on the decision, the reactions of different auditors to this situation will differ, and they are likely to be influenced by considerations other than the significance of the findings, such as the "time available for testing inventory."

Suppose, again, that the auditor examines sales invoices by comparing them with entries in the sales journal. He examines 120 items and finds that one invoice has been entered erroneously and the customer has been charged less than the amount appearing on the invoice, which is the proper amount. All the other transactions appear to be properly recorded. What does this indicate about the accuracy of the bookkeeping? What conclusion should be drawn about the entries not examined? If one such error can occur, others can also. The object of the sampling, or testing, is to discover the general condition of the accounts. What does this specific finding indicate? The answers to this and the foregoing questions can be given objectively upon the basis of statistical reasoning, and after the fundamental form of such reasoning has been developed in the following sections, answers to these specific questions and others like them will be suggested.

PROBABILITY AND STATISTICAL INFERENCE

Statistical sampling theory is based upon the computation of probabilities. The term "probability" is commonly used in a variety of senses, but in statistical sampling theory its mathematical meaning is: "the ratio of certain events to all the possible events in a series or set." Thus, if we were to calculate the probability of drawing the ace of spades from a hand containing the four aces we would divide 1 (the number of possible events giving us the ace of spades) by 4 (the sum of all the possible events, corresponding to the four cards, as four possibilities) and we would get 1/4, or 0.25. Everyone knows that the "chances" of getting the ace of spades in this case are 1 in 4; the basic concept of probability is a familiar one.

In sampling processes the computation of probabilities is used to enable the operator to come to some conclusion about the thing sampled (the "population") without assuming that the sample gives an exactly representative picture of the group from which it came, and by using only rigorous, objective reasoning. Let us suppose that a shipment of electric light bulbs is received which, according to the manufacturer's statement, has a maximum of 10 per cent of bulbs that will fail to burn 500 hours. We wish to decide whether or not to accept the shipment (the population, in this case) by taking a sample of 25 bulbs and testing them to determine how long they will burn. Suppose that we do so, and that we discover 8 of them fail to burn 500 hours. If the shipment contained 1,000 bulbs, of which exactly 100 would fail to burn 500 hours, it is obvious that our sample could have contained 25 such inferior bulbs or any number of them from 0 to 25. The significance of the particular number drawn (i.e., 8 in 25) can be assessed only through the computation of the probability of drawing this particular sample from a population of 1,000 that was 10 per cent defective (in the sense that 10 per cent of the members would burn less than 500 hours). Mathematical means are available, of course, for computing this: a random sample of 25 from a population 10 per cent defective will contain 8 defectives 0.180 per cent of the time, and it will contain that number or fewer defectives 99.954 per cent of the time.[1] Since with samples of 25 from populations 10 per cent defective we will have less than 8 defectives 99.9 per cent of the time, the presence of 8 defectives in this case indicates that we have a very rare sample from such a population or *that the population is not in fact only 10 per cent defective.* We would therefore reject the shipment, reasoning that it was not likely to be only 10 per cent defective in view of the quality of the sample drawn. In other words, we may appraise a population from a sample by: first, making an estimate of the population's quality; second, calculating the probability of drawing the sample from a population of such quality; and third, accepting or rejecting the estimate according to whether the sample is a common or a rare one from a population of the estimated character. In the example of the light bulbs we took the manufacturer's estimate of the population, but it is not necessary to make an estimate which is expected to reflect a judgment on the particular population. We may instead set up a standard that the population will be required to meet and make it

---

[1] These probability computations are made by use of the binomial distribution and are approximate for the case cited.

our estimate, or, in more technical language, hypothesis. If the sample actually drawn would, by a computation of probability, frequently be drawn from the standard population or from the postulated population, the actual population would be accepted as likely to be close to the standard one.

The process of reasoning outlined above requires the establishment of a level of probability upon which the decision is to be made as well as a hypothesis or standard which will represent acceptable as against unacceptable quality. Where no outside restrictions are imposed, every operator may choose his own probability level (as each auditor decides by his own standards to accept or reject a set of accounting entries as accurate or not) ; but professional statisticians have generally used levels of 90 per cent to 99 per cent as a basis for decisions. If a like sample would be drawn from the postulated population (hypothetical population used as a standard) only 10 per cent or less of the time, or perhaps 1 per cent or less of the time, they would reject the hypothesis upon which probability was calculated as not likely to be of the character of the real population from which the sample was in fact drawn. As the level of probability on which the decision rests is raised, the cost of sampling also rises, and as the probability level used is reduced, the risk of accepting substandard populations as standard or better increases. A level of 90 per cent for auditing applications is tentatively suggested here as consistent with economy and reliability.

Just as the customer decided to accept or reject the shipment of light bulbs by determining the number of defectives in a sample, the auditor may decide, upon the basis of the number of erroneous items in a sample, to accept as sufficiently accurate any accounting population of entries, computations, or postings, or to reject them as requiring either further investigation or a qualified certificate. By setting a standard in terms of the maximum percentage of errors to be accepted without further testing, a sample of the area may be interpreted in the light of the probability of drawing it from the postulated (standard) population, or hypothesis. This gives the auditor an objective, mathematical basis for the interpretation of his sample;

it also provides means of determining the minimum sample size and permits other statistical operations, as this volume in subsequent sections indicates. Prominent among the advantages of statistical reasoning in auditing are the possibilities of better control over the cost of auditing and the establishment of general standards for the quantity of auditing work to be done in major areas of the accounts; both these possibilities flow from the opportunity to compute minimum sample sizes.[2] The limitations of the method for auditing, as well as more complete development of its application, are the subjects of succeeding chapters; the present objective is to show that statistical sampling theory is usable as a tool of auditing.

THE LIKELIHOOD RATIO

In discussing statistical reasoning in the preceding section we had recourse to a single probability computation; that is, the probability of drawing a particular sample from a postulated population. Obviously a great variety of samples may be drawn from any particular large population, and many of them will be drawn with such frequency or probability that the actual population would be accepted as not materially different from any common standard which might be used. This leaves much room for variation between actual quality of the population sampled and the standard quality desired. It is desirable to make the process more discriminating, and, particularly, to reduce the risk of accepting a population much poorer than the standard one. This can be done by means of the likelihood ratio.

The likelihood ratio is a ratio of two probabilities. Although this suggests complications, the method is actually very easy to use in practice since published tables that reduce the computations to simple arithmetic are available. The two probabilities used in calculating a likelihood ratio are derived from two different hypotheses or standard populations. One of these hypotheses represents a desirable condition in the population, or, for our purposes, the accounts. The other represents an undesirable condition—a condition which would require the auditor to qualify his certificate or to under-

[2] See appendix i for a further discussion of the nature of statistical sampling theory.

take a very intensive examination of the particular area. When a sample is drawn from an actual population, the probability of drawing it from *each* of the two hypothetical populations is calculated, and these two probabilities are brought together as the numerator and denominator of a fraction. Let us make the probability of drawing our sample from the undesirable population the numerator and the probability of drawing it from the desirable population the denominator. Then if the fraction is 9 (the probability of getting the sample from the undesirable population is nine times as great as the probability of getting it from the desirable one), we would conclude that the actual population from which the sample came was much more *likely* to be of the character of the undesirable hypothesis (or standard of measurement) than to be of the character of the desirable one. On the other hand, if the fraction were 1/9, or 0.111 +, we would conclude that the actual population was more *likely* of the character of the desirable hypothesis and so accept it as satisfactory, since the probability of drawing it from the desirable population is nine times as great as the probability of getting it from the undesirable one. Probability levels other than 9 and 1/9 may be used; 9.5 and 1/7.2 could be used if desired. As in any application of probability in sampling theory, the use of the likelihood ratio does not attempt to say precisely what is the percentage of errors (to use the auditing situation) in the actual population. This could be done, as a matter of fact, only by examining all the items in the population. It does enable the auditor to come to a conclusion about the actual population on rational, objective grounds; it enables him to make a decision by use of rigorous mathematical reasoning that the particular area of the accounting is or is not apparently satisfactorily accurate. A more formal description of the likelihood ratio is given in appendix ii.

SEQUENTIAL SAMPLING

Use of the likelihood ratio as a practical tool is made easy by the development of sequential sampling. This method was developed during World War II by the Statistical Research Group of the Applied Mathematics Panel of the National Defense Research Committee.[3] To realize the ease with which the method may be applied the reader need only refer to table 10 (appendix ii, p. 91). The number in the sample is read from the column headed n; the number of defects which may appear in the sample and still permit accept- ance of the actual population as more likely to be of the character of the desirable hypothesis is given in the column headed y_1; the number of defects in the sample which dictate a conclusion that the actual population is more likely to be of the character of the unde- sirable hypothesis is given in the column headed y_2. Accordingly, if in an actual auditing case we were using the values for which the left half of this table is drawn up and we had taken a sample or "test" of 239 vouchers, we would draw conclusions as follows: accept the vouchers as satisfactory if no errors or only one or two errors were found (assuming that the errors were clerical, and not frauds, of course) ; reject the vouchers as unsatisfactory if five or more errors are found (and inform the client that more time will have to be spent on vouchers or that the certificate must be qualified) since the sample indicates they contain more than the allowable maximum of errors; and if the number of defects falls between two and five we conclude that the evidence is not sufficient to justify a decision in either direc- tion, the usual result of which is to increase the size of the sample to accumulate more evidence. It should be noted that a sample of 89 with no errors would permit acceptance; this indicates that, where the accounts are in a satisfactory condition, auditing samples may often be smaller than has usually been assumed. This would permit closer, more deliberate scrutiny of the fewer items as against the rapid checking of a mass of them, and would improve the auditor's chance to recognize subtle errors.

The method may be approached through its graphical form. The procedure consists of drawing the graph for the values desired (the two hypotheses between which choice is to be made and the levels of

[3] The underlying mathematical work is that of A. Wald and is presented by the Statisti- cal Research Group of Columbia University in its report: *Sequential Analysis of Statistical Data: Theory* (S. R. G. Report 75, AMP Report 30.1, September, 1943). The applications are discussed in S. R. G. Report 255, AMP Report 30.2R, July, 1944: *Sequential Analysis in Inspection and Experimentation,* and in *Sampling Inspection* (New York, 1948).

probability, or components of the likelihood ratio which are chosen) and simply plotting the results as the items in the sample are drawn The figure shows the general form of the graph.

The number in the sample is plotted on the x axis and the number of defects discovered is plotted on the y axis. As soon as the plotted line falls below the lower of the two parallel lines, the sampling stops and the desirable hypothesis is accepted as the one to which the actual population is more closely related; if the line runs above the upper of the two parallel lines, the undesirable hypothesis is taken

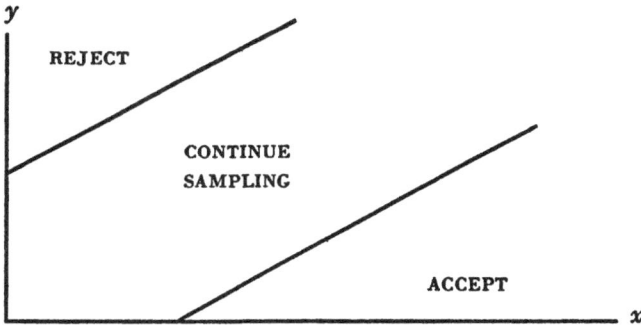

as descriptive of the population; and if the line remains within the two parallel lines, the evidence is inconclusive and the sample must be enlarged before a decision can be made. It should be noted that this procedure minimizes the sample required by the circumstances of each case, since the sampling is stopped as soon as the evidence is sufficient to warrant a decision; this, of course, is the basis for the name of the method. A more complete discussion of sequential sampling is given in appendix ii, pages 87–93.

The particular values given in table 10 were chosen by the author as appropriate to auditing conditions. The left half of the table shows at what points decisions to accept or reject an area of the accounts as satisfactory or unsatisfactory may be made, when the desirable condition is defined as the presence of not more than 0.5 per cent of errors, the undesirable condition is defined as the presence of 3 per cent or more of errors, and when it is agreed to run a risk of error in accepting the desirable hypothesis when the other one is true of not more than 10 per cent and of improperly rejecting the desirable hypothesis of 5 per cent. The "risks" refer to the level of probability on which the decision is made. The right half of the table uses the same risks but increases the spread between the hypotheses; this also reduces the size of the minimum sample. Further discussion of the sequential sampling method is given in appendix ii where formulas are given for computing the figures for a table such as table 10 or for drawing the graph, illustrated on page 9, for any desired value. Attention is also called to table 12 (appendix ii, p. 93), which gives the minimum sample sizes for acceptance and rejection of a population and average sample sizes, assuming either one or the other of the hypotheses to be correct, for a considerable number of possible hypotheses, and which therefore permits the reader to see the implications of using particular values.

ANSWERS TO QUESTIONS ON PAGES 2 AND 3

In the first section of this chapter, two auditing samples were described and questions of their significance were posed. In the intervening sections it has been indicated that these questions may be answered on the basis of the probabilities of the samples being drawn from groups of accounting entries or computations of desirable as against undesirable quality. Specific answers may be given to the questions by using the values represented in the left half of table 10. The first case dealt with an inventory of 1,200 items of which the auditor made a test count of 90, finding 3 of the items so tested to have significant errors. The table indicates that the inventory is likely to have 3 per cent or more of errors, and where this is so it would be necessary to increase the sample to 303 without finding another error if the inventory is to be accepted. If the values of the right half of the table are used, the sample would be raised to 201. The second case involved a sample of 120 sales invoices of which one was entered for less than the proper amount. Reference to the table shows this evidence to be inconclusive, since zero errors are necessary for acceptance of a sample of 120, whereas it may not be rejected unless 4 are present. If the sample were increased to 160

without disclosure of another error, it would be accepted as indicative of a satisfactory condition in the accounts. Should reference be
made to the right half of the table in this case, the original sample of
120 with one error would have given the basis for acceptance, but to
reach this conclusion it would have been necessary to take a sample
of only 100.

CHAPTER **II**

Auditing Conditions and
Statistical Devices

Auditing Conditions and Probability Inferences

THE EXAMPLES given in the preceding chapter have indicated the nature of the methods for application of statistical sampling theory to auditing procedure. The results of auditing tests were summarized in terms of the number of defective, or erroneous, items found in a sample. It would be desirable to summarize results in terms of the money value of errors in the population, but this does not seem to be a very practicable objective. Accounting errors arise almost entirely from human fallibility, and there is no regular or simple pattern of human fallibilities on which probability calculations could be based. The specific settings in which errors can occur are indefinitely great, ranging from the misplacing of a decimal point to the misconception of an accounting principle. Furthermore, whatever the force which causes an error to be made (as fatigue of a worker), there is no simple relationship which connects it with the amount of the resulting error. An error from a misplaced decimal point depends in amount on the distance of misplacement and the digits involved, which vary almost at random.

Since a statistical interpretation of continuous variables cannot be adapted to auditing, we use what the statistician terms sampling by attributes. This is a matter of using a twofold or binomial classification, "satisfactory" and "not satisfactory," instead of a continuous scale of measurement. Wherever auditing samples are taken, the items observed may be classified as correct or incorrect and the process of reasoning outlined previously may be used as a basis for acceptance or other action with reference to the group from which

[12]

the sample was drawn. This is possible because we know from mathematical reasoning the exact distribution of samples of any size drawn from any population described in a twofold classification; in other words, we can calculate exactly the probability that a particular sample would be drawn by chance alone from a particular population.

It can be seen, then, that auditing conditions are an appropriate field for the application of statistical methods. The areas in which such methods are appropriate are those in which the sampling technique is already applied in auditing. They consist of the original records and calculations, the books of original entry derived from the original records, and to areas such as inventory and accounts receivable where a considerable volume of detail exists. At present, auditors consider the nature of the errors found and subjectively consider the probability that others may exist in the unexamined section of the entries. The use of statistical inference will make this probability computation explicit and permit the establishment of unequivocal auditing standards with respect to the extent of sampling.

APPROPRIATENESS OF BINOMIAL DISTRIBUTION FOR AUDITING CONCLUSIONS

When samples from finite populations are to be interpreted by means of the binomial distribution, it is necessary to replace, in effect, each item drawn before the next one is drawn. This is true because when drawing from a finite population it is essential to the strict validity of the mathematics that the proportion of good and bad remain constant; in other words, it is necessary that each drawing be made from a population in which, say, 10 per cent of the items are white and 90 per cent black. If a second item is drawn without replacing the first one, the second would not have been drawn from a population 10 per cent white and the probabilities would be slightly (in a single instance of this sort, insignificantly) altered.[1] Three observations

---

[1] The computation of probabilities where the drawing is made from a binomial population without replacement may be accurately made by the formula for the hypergeometric distribution. This is: $Pw,b = \dfrac{W^c w \cdot B^c b}{N^c n}$, where Pw,b is the probability of getting w white

are to be made concerning the significance of this situation for auditing uses.

First, as will be more completely explained in chapter v, it is possible to draw and tabulate samples so as to satisfy the formalities of the mathematics (by use of random sampling numbers).

Second, there will be many instances in auditing in which the size of the sample relative to the lot which is being sampled will be small, and under such circumstances the fact that the sample may be drawn without replacement may be ignored because the error involved is so small as to be of no significance. As a general working rule, it may be said that the sample should be not larger than 10 per cent of the population if this viewpoint is to be adopted.

Third, it may be argued that, since the ideal condition for the application of the binomial sampling distribution is one in which the population sampled is infinite, auditing conditions may be conceived as presenting an infinite population. In an infinite population which has 10 per cent white and 90 per cent black balls, for example, the withdrawal of any finite number of balls will not change the proportions remaining, since there is no limit to the number of balls which can be withdrawn. This condition may be said to exist wherever there is a continuous process which produces members of the population, or where the total *possible* membership is infinite. An example of the former is to be found in manufacturing processes which are carried on indefinitely, and illustration of the latter may be seen in the growing of samples of grass—the number actually growing and possible of being grown is infinite. In auditing, the process of recording transactions may be looked upon as providing an infinite number of calculations and entries (as the weary worker often conceives them). Accordingly, it is conceivable for the auditor to take the attitude that, in examining the inventory at a particular date, he is drawing a sample from a population of continuing in-

---

balls and b black balls in a sample of n taken from a population of W white balls and B black balls without replacement in the process of drawing any particular sample of n. Of course, $w + b = n$ and $W + B = N$, the latter being the total number of items in the population. The numerical evaluation of this formula for any considerable range of samples, ratio of W and values of N, is so laborious that no general tables of it are available.

ventory calculations (made annually) and so test the hypothesis that the process is carried on with a ratio of errors of, say, 3 per cent. From this viewpoint the binomial distribution is formally appropriate.

There is some support for the last observation from other than purely statistical considerations. Obviously, continuity is characteristic of business and other financial operations. This fact has been given emphasis by the accounting profession in at least two ways: recent literature has frequently been concerned with the problems of calculation of periodic income, the usual conclusion being that reliance upon the statements of any one year alone is to be avoided; and public accountants have adopted the attitude that consistency in accounting methods is of more consequence than the use of any one (of alternative) principles, and have gone to the length of referring to this view in their certificates. The following sentence has been officially suggested and its form widely used in the auditor's short-form report: "In our opinion, the accompanying balance-sheet and related statements of income and surplus present fairly the position of the XYZ Company at April 30, 1939, and the results of its operations for the fiscal year, in conformity with generally accepted principles applied on a basis *consistent with that of the preceding year.*" (Italics mine.)[2] Since for general purposes the profession looks upon the accounts it deals with as continuing processes, it may appropriately use the same criterion for statistical purposes.

The viewpoint expressed in the foregoing paragraph is to be contrasted with the narrower one that the sampling relates only to a particular fiscal year, so that the population sampled in the case of inventory would consist only of the computations made for that subject at the closing date in question. This narrower approach seems more desirable in auditing work. Where the concern examined is newly organized, or where the auditor's relationship to the client is only beginning, it is obvious that there cannot be a feeling of assurance on the part of the auditor that a continuity of operations, satis-

---

[2] See *Extensions of Auditing Procedure,* Committee on Auditing Procedure, American Institute of Accountants (New York, 1939), and *The Revised S.E.C. Rule on "Accountants' Certificates,"* American Institute of Accountants (New York, 1941).

factory for statistical inference of the type suggested, actually exists. Furthermore, personnel and methods change from year to year so that the concept of a constant set of causal factors breaks down. It is not recommended that the third concept (i.e., that the population sampled is infinite) be used in auditing; it is mentioned here because it has been used in some biological experiments and the analogy to auditing may occur to some readers.

In very exceptional cases (as where fraud is suspected) the sampling technique may be abandoned; it may be used and interpreted as a binomial distribution of the narrow population in hand if the size of the sample can appropriately be small relative to the population (a limit of 10 per cent has been suggested); or so large a proportion of the population may be inspected as to permit the assumption that the quality of the whole is virtually identical with that of the items observed; and, finally, sampling with replacement (by use of random sampling numbers, for example) will make any population effectively infinite.

It is of importance to note that the percentage of defective entries in a set of accounts is not the element of primary importance in judging the quality of the accounts. Two per cent of insignificant errors would have less influence on the auditor's decision to accept the accounts than one-half of one per cent of seriously erroneous entries would have. It is not so important to establish the specific percentage of error in the population as to estimate generally the quality of the work done in creating the entries; in other words, to determine whether a reasonable degree of accounting control appears to exist in fact. For this purpose the percentage of errors is significant as one index or one of several measures of quality, since a relatively large number of errors indicates poor work and suggests that errors existing in the unobserved portion of the population, occurring beyond the limits of adequate control, may be, in individual instances, of serious amount. The use of this index of quality in auditing is suggested here because it is of significance in itself and because it is amenable to statistical analysis. That it cannot be all-inclusive in its solution of the auditor's problems should not deny it the role it can usefully play. The use of statistical methods will add to the auditor's equipment an objective basis for assessing the quality of the internal check and control and the quality of the accounting effort generally, thus improving a process or method of examination of accounts which is already firmly established.

The Auditor's Courses of Action from Statistical Inference

There are three courses open to the auditor upon discovery that a particular sample does not support the hypothesis of a satisfactory population. These are: (1) take more samples of the population; (2) refuse to issue a certificate; (3) issue a qualified certificate. Of course he may also make recommendations for the improvement of internal check and control.

The first course may be taken where an unqualified certificate is desired, and will be the appropriate action in most cases. Enlarging the sample will dispose of those cases in which a very rare, and therefore unrepresentative, sample is drawn from a satisfactory population, and where the population is actually unsatisfactory the sampling would usually automatically continue until all or nearly all of the entries under review were examined, in which case the errors of substance could be adjusted.

The second and third courses are available where the client's wishes preclude as extensive sampling as is necessary for an unqualified report. They present no new principle in auditing practice, since the necessity for qualification—or, in extreme cases, refusal of any statement of opinion—has long been recognized where the scope of the audit is restricted by the client.

Statistical methods, especially if they be established as standard practice, place the auditor in a much stronger position for making recommendations relative to internal check and for justifying a qualification. In the first place, an objective measure of the performance of the accounting staff is given in the probability of drawing a sample with a certain number of defectives from a satisfactory population; and, second, it can be very graphically shown that poor performances require the taking of more samples than do good ones, thus increasing the cost of auditing. Obviously a specific measurable standard places the auditor in a much more comfortable position in making qualifications, since it relieves him of the suspicion of caprice or overly meticulous judgment, and, of more consequence, relieves him of most of the pressure to make a more favorable report than he would like to make by placing responsibility for the decisions upon impersonal mathematical principles and the general standard of the profession.

SPECIFIC STATISTICAL DEVICES FOR AUDITING

Four statistical devices are here suggested as useful for auditing purposes:

1. Judgment of a series or set of entries or computations from a random sample by the likelihood ratio.

2. Determination of sample size.

3. Tests for accounting control.

4. Test for bias in the direction of error.

JUDGMENT OF GROUP FROM RANDOM SAMPLE

The first "device" listed is the fundamental process, and its application to auditing has been outlined in the foregoing pages, and is more fully detailed in appendix ii. The procedure is to select a sample and to consider whether it would be likely to have been drawn from a satisfactory as against an unsatisfactory population.

It is not necessary that the hypothesis about the character of the population be a close estimate of the actual population; we may use instead the hypothesis that the population is at least of standard quality. If it is in fact better, the probability of judging it adequate is increased, since fewer defective items will be drawn than would be drawn from the hypothetical population. If the actual population is worse than the alternative hypothesis, it will show more defectives than the established maximum in all but very rare cases (assuming a high level of probability is used in the interpretation).

Where the actual population falls between the two hypotheses the results depend on the relative proximity to the two alternatives set up.

In drawing conclusions from the likelihood ratio we must of course take some risk of error if the sampling procedure is to be at all economical. This fact is inherent in the sampling process generally; where certainty is essential, sampling must always be, in some degree, inadequate. When probability computations can be made, however, the sample can be devised to correspond with the degree of risk which we are willing to assume. This must be determined in the light of the size of sample which results and of the cost of drawing and examining the items in the sample. Table 12 (appendix ii) gives average sample sizes resulting from the use of various hypotheses which the author feels cover the range of magnitude suitable to auditing use. The risks reflected in the table are considered appropriate to general use by statisticians, and they are tentatively recommended for auditing. In this case the risks mean that once in twenty drawings we will get from a satisfactory population a sample with so many errors in it as to lead us to believe that it came from an unsatisfactory population ($\alpha = 0.05$); and once in ten times we will get from an unsatisfactory population a sample with so few errors as to lead us to believe that it came from a satisfactory population. The only consequence of drawing a sample which calls for rejection of the population when the population is actually satisfactory, so far as auditing use is concerned, will usually be the taking of some more items to enlarge the sample, which will disclose the exceptional character of the first drawings. The acceptance of unsatisfactory populations as satisfactory will sometimes occur, as it must with any sampling procedure. With probability computations this can be controlled at whatever level is desired; without them it will occur upon an unpredictable pattern. It is to be emphasized in this connection that an unsatisfactory population will be accepted once in, say, ten times *when it exists*, and not once in ten audits (most of the populations presumably will be satisfactory), and when it does happen it does not necessarily mean that the whole result of an audit will be wrong. The latter conclusion arises from the fact that the sampling technique will be applied to individual areas of the accounts, and a single unsatisfactory area does not destroy the accounting statements. It would presumably mean that a qualification which should be made would be missed or that errors which would otherwise have been ferreted out and adjusted were overlooked.

The foregoing suggests consideration of the relative costs of auditing (drawing and examining samples) and the consequences of rejecting lots which are really satisfactory and of accepting lots which are in fact not satisfactory. This subject will be considered in chapter iv. It is also to be noted that we have assumed that we are dealing with random samples which may be tentatively defined at this point as samples in which each member of the parent population has an equal chance to appear. It will be apparent at once to every professional accountant that auditing samples do not always satisfy this definition; the questions which this situation raises will be considered in chapter v.

DETERMINATION OF SAMPLE SIZE

The process of determining the size of sample to be taken follows closely upon the computations previously made. We may set a minimum sample at once by noting the minimum sample required to permit an acceptance of the population. This can be observed for a considerable number of values of the variables in table 12 (appendix ii), and more may be seen in table 2.23 of S. R. G. Report 255. The minimum sample necessary to permit acceptance of a population may be computed for any values of the variables by solving the equation of sequential sampling as described in appendix ii. In terms of the graphical representation (see chap. i), this is the first point at which we are able to arrive which falls in the area we have labeled "accept." Obviously if we are actually to make an acceptance upon the basis of a minimum sample it must be drawn without disclosing any error.

Another basis for selecting a minimum sample is to specify that the sample shall be large enough to disclose one defective item upon a selected probability level, given an hypothesis as to the population from which it is drawn. This refers to a simple probability computation from the binomial distribution. Reference to table 9 (appendix i) illustrates this for the case of drawing balls from a bowl. It shows that we can expect to draw at least one white ball in approximately 73 per cent of the samples of 25 we take from a population 10 per cent white. When we have a chart showing the minimum number of defectives we can expect to see in samples of various sizes drawn from populations of various ratios of defectives, we can read off the sample size necessary to enable us to see at least one defective in a population of whatever ratio of defectives we wish to take as a standard.[3] Results from such calculations are roughly equivalent to those obtained from the formulas for sequential sampling. For example, the minimum sample necessary to see one defective when drawing from a population 3 per cent defective, if a risk of 10 per cent is to be taken, is 75; upon a sequential sampling basis where p_1 is .0001 (near to zero), p_2 is 0.03, $\alpha = 0.10$ and $\beta = 0.10$, the minimum sample required is 73. In view of the desirability of using the likelihood ratio as the basis for the general evaluation of auditing samples and the ease with which it may be applied through the use of the sequential sampling formulas, it is recommended that minimum sample sizes be set upon the presumption that sequential sampling will be used.[4] However, should it be desired to set a minimum sample size as an auditing standard apart from statistical interpretation of the sample once it is drawn, the task may be done most readily upon the basis of a single hypothesis as to the maximum percentage of errors contemplated and some probability level—say

---

[3] Such charts have been prepared by Leslie E. Simon for the 90 per cent and 99.5 per cent probability levels and are published in the appendix to his book, *An Engineer's Manual of Statistical Methods* (New York, 1941).

[4] The only thoroughgoing effort to apply mathematical probability theory to auditing procedure which the present writer was able to find when this work was begun was undertaken to determine the sample size necessary to observe one fraudulent entry, given an absolute number of fraudulent entries as an hypothesis. It uses the formulas for combinations, and through a process of approximation, arrives at samples expressed as percentages of the population. The sample sizes arrived at are not very different from those obtained by the methods of the present work, but no attempt was made in the other material to make a general interpretation of the sample. See Lewis A. Carman, "The Efficacy of Tests," *The American Accountant*, XVIII (Dec., 1933), 360–366.

90 per cent. For purposes of auditing standards, the question of the interpretation of the sample may be divorced from the question of minimum size, in which case the minimum may be specified in terms of a single binomial distribution. Furthermore, the minimum may in such case require a sufficient sample so as to give a certain assurance that 2 or 3 or any desired number of defectives would be seen in a population of specified quality.

At this point it should be observed that considerations of sample size in binomial conditions include no reference to the size of the population sampled. This follows from the mathematical character of the distribution, which assumes merely that the drawing is made from a population in which the percentage of defectives is constant. As observed previously, this condition requires that in practice the auditor must be satisfied to look upon the population as a continuous, and therefore infinite, one, or that he sample with replacement, or that he use a sample sufficiently small relative to the lot in hand so that the error involved in drawing without replacement from a finite population and interpreting upon the basis of the binomial may be ignored. Whatever the means by which the logic of binomial conditions is satisfied, the important conclusion is that the absolute size of the sample is the important element in judging the effectiveness of the sample to disclose one or some other number of defectives upon the selected probability basis. This conclusion is definitely at variance with auditing practice at many points of the auditing process, since it is common practice to set the size of the sample as a ratio of the entries or computations made in the period under review. The following quotation from a prominent text on auditing procedure indicates common practice in the verification of inventory extensions:

For example, the senior may issue instructions that all extensions of items of inventory which are in excess of $1,000.00 be verified, and that all extensions between $1,000.00 and $500.00 be verified to the nearest $10.00, and that three extensions on each inventory page involving totals of less than $500.00 be verified to the nearest $1.00. In this procedure, an extensive test would be made of the extensions involving inventories. As opposed to the extensive test just outlined, and if the staff of the client had been reasonably accurate in its computation of inventories, the senior may instruct the junior to select at random any five items on each sheet and verify them to the last cent.[5]

Following this instruction, more entries would be examined in a large inventory (large in number of items) than in a small one, but statistical reasoning does not require this. It is only necessary that a random sample of certain *absolute* size be taken in order to judge whether a particular lot probably meets the specification set up in the population used as a hypothesis.

To some degree, however, auditing practice seems to have recognized that proportionally larger samples are not required in larger concerns. By personal observation and discussions with colleagues in the profession, the present author has become aware that in audits of very large and complicated operations emphasis, so far as all routine bookkeeping processes are concerned, has in recent years been placed almost entirely on ascertaining that the accounting methods set up were adequate in principle and were in fact being used, so that detailed verification had become a relatively minor part of the work on such engagements. There has always been a tendency on the part of competent auditors to test a larger proportion of the entries in a very small concern than they tested in a relatively large one. Both of these practices are justified by considerations of internal check and control, which is likely to be effective in proportion to the volume of operations. Within the very broad middle ground, which is the area of the typical audit, the previous observation reflects common practice. This means that in many cases a considerable decrease may be made in the size of samples taken in audits where the accounts are kept with an acceptable degree of accuracy.

TESTS FOR ACCOUNTING CONTROL

It is possible to extend the procedure for the testing or interpretation of auditing samples by calculating the probability that samples differing as much or more than those under observation would have been drawn from the postulated population. This computation is

---

[5] Arthur W. Holmes, *Auditing Principles and Procedure* (rev. ed.; Chicago, 1945), pp. 102–103.

made in scientific work to aid in answering the question whether
there is evidence to deny the assumption that a series of experiments
was carried on under constant conditions, and is sometimes referred
to as a test for statistical control, which term for present use may
be metamorphosed into "accounting control." However, a different
basis for distinguishing lack of control seems preferable in auditing
work.

Suppose, for example, that an inventory was taken by two distinct
crews, and that a sample of 100 items has been examined from the
work of each crew. In the sample of 200 there are 4 errors. Reference to table 10 indicates that the sample is inconclusive as to the
hypothesis that the population is either 0.005 defective or better or
0.03 defective or worse. Since we cannot make a choice between
these alternatives, the need to take more samples is suggested, an
unqualified certificate being desired. Where there is some basis in
fact for the belief that conditions differed in the preparation of different sections of the transactions or computations under test, the
sample can be divided and the two parts considered separately. It
was noted above that 100 items were checked from the work of each
of two crews. Let us presume that one group of 100 contained none
of the errors. Separate consideration of these as two samples of 100
in the left section of table 10 discloses that the one with 4 errors
indicates an unsatisfactory population. This suggests that we con-
centrate attention upon the work of the crew from which the sample
with 4 errors came; since a sample with 4 errors would have to contain 374 items to be acceptable under the hypotheses used, it would
be appropriate to notify the client that a recheck by his own staff
of the work in question appeared necessary; sufficient sampling by
the auditor to settle definitely the question of the acceptability of the
computations would probably be uneconomical.[6] We thus have a
means of distinguishing areas of the accounts which may not follow

---

[6] If the basis for judging auditing samples seems unduly restrictive as a result of this
illustration, the reader should recall that the results may be adjusted to a basis considered economical by the profession through definition of the nature and, if desired, the
amount (absolute or relative) of individual errors to be tabulated as such, and through
the setting of the levels of risk as well as by selection of the hypotheses between which
choice is to be made.

the same patterns or be created under the same conditions as other similar areas, which gives objectivity to our decision.

The foregoing is not the conventional basis for a test of statistical control; as was noted in the first paragraph of the present section, the test regularly consists of a computation of the probability of drawing two samples as divergent as the ones in hand from a postulated population. This requires a single hypothesis as to the parent population, and opens the way to the acceptance of two samples from different populations as coming from one when the two actual populations are not very far apart. Upon the basis of greater discrimination, therefore, the separate interpretation by the likelihood ratio of parts of a sample which may reflect different conditions is recommended. The use of the single hypothesis method will be described in the following section where its application is more appropriate.

TEST FOR BIAS IN DIRECTION OF ERROR

In rare cases it may be useful to get a mathematical indication on the question of bias in the direction of error. To take an illustration from inventory accounting once more, let us suppose that in examining the pricing of a wholesale hardware inventory (which contains thousands of items) the sample discloses 10 errors which tend to overstate the inventory and 32 which tend to understate it (i.e., 10 positive and 32 negative errors). The question to be decided is this: does the preponderance of negative errors indicate that the inventory errors *in toto* are predominantly negative in direction, or could we expect in, say, 90 per cent of the random drawings from a population where positive and negative errors were equal in number, to get such a distribution in our sample so that we could attribute this particular sample to chance? In other words, is this a reasonably common random sample from a population in which the numbers of errors are qual in terms of direction?

Since we are restricted to a single hypothesis here (i.e., equal numbers of errors in the two directions), we may use the normal variate to calculate the probability of drawing the particular sample.

The normal variate indicates the probability of drawing two particular samples from a given population. The computation is made by the following formula.

$$NV = \frac{r - nq}{\sqrt{npq}}$$

where

NV = normal variate
  r = number of errors in the sample in the predominant direction
  n = number of errors found in the sample *in toto*
  p and q each = 0.5 (the proportion of errors falling in either direction in the hypothetical population)

For the illustration suggested, the calculation of the normal variate is as follows.

$$NV = \frac{32 - (42)\ (0.5)}{\sqrt{42\ (0.5)\ (0.5)}} = \frac{11}{\sqrt{10.5}} = \frac{11}{3.24} = 3.4$$

In calculating NV the sign of the numerator is not significant and is therefore usually written as positive. The value of NV must be converted into an expression of probability in order for its meaning to be clear; this may be done sufficiently well for auditing purposes with table 1.

It can be seen from table 1 that samples which give a normal variate of 2 or less would be drawn from the postulated population by chance 95 per cent of the time, and may therefore be accepted as likely coming from a population not essentially different from the postulated one. In a normal variate of 3 or more, on the other hand, the probability is 3 in 1,000 or less that such a sample will be drawn from the postulated population, and we are therefore entitled to doubt that it did in fact come from such a population. Use of the formula for 48 errors in which 18 are positive and 30 are negative gives an NV of 1.73, which table 1 indicates would be exceeded in 5 to 13 per cent of random drawings from a population in which errors are equally divided in direction. In such a case we would not conclude that the sample indicated any predominance of negative errors.

TABLE 1

PROBABILITY (*P*) OF DRAWING A RARER SAMPLE THAN THOSE
GIVING THE NORMAL VARIATES (*NV*) LISTED

NV	*P*
0.5	0.62
1.0	0.32
1.5	0.13
2.0	0.05
2.5	0.01
3.0	0.003

This device gives a basis for investigation of possible deliberate understatement or overstatement of inventory prices where it is possible, or at least economical, to proceed only upon a sampling basis. It would give the auditor an impersonal defense for a decision to qualify the certificate with respect to inventory in such a case.

CHAPTER **III**

Applications to Specific
Accounts

THE PROBABILITY LEVEL AND HYPOTHESES ABOUT
RATIO OF ERRORS

IN ESTABLISHING a probability level for the interpretation of auditing samples, consideration must be given to the conflicting demands
of accuracy on the one hand and cost on the other. If a 90 per cent
level is chosen, the sample will show more than the maximum per-
missible errors (when it was in fact drawn from an acceptable population) 10 per cent of the time. This will lead to the taking of
additional samples (when they are not required) 10 per cent of
the time. A 99.5 per cent level would result in this difficulty only
0.5 per cent of the time. As was previously noted in this connection,
the higher level of probability requires a larger minimum sample
and a larger sample for any specified number of defectives than
does the 90 per cent basis. The cost of sampling is therefore increased. The subject of the cost of auditing will be considered again
in chapter iv; the probability level is mentioned at the present junc-
ture as a basis for the levels used in the discussion of the case materials which are included in the present chapter. The probability
levels referred to in this connection are $\alpha = 0.05$ and $\beta = 0.10$, that
is, a risk of 5 per cent that the population will be considered unsatisfactory when it is in fact acceptable, and a risk of 10 per cent
that it will be accepted when it is in fact of unacceptable character.[1]
These values are used in the present work because they have been
used to a considerable degree by professional statisticians and be-

[1] For further discussion of the terms α and β and related elements of the likelihood
ratio and sequential sampling, see appendix ii.

cause they seem to the author to be appropriate to auditing conditions. It must be emphasized, however, that the profession may prefer to select different probability levels to suit different ideas of economy in sampling, and that this freedom applies also to the selection of standard hypotheses upon which the sampling proceeds.

In setting the ratios of erorrs for the hypothetical populations between which choice is to be made of an estimate of the population in hand, it is of course necessary that the population deemed acceptable be one which auditors generally can agree is satisfactory and that the alternative hypothesis be one which can generally be agreed upon as representing unacceptable conditions. In this connection it has already been noted that the only measure of accounting performance which seems amenable to statistical sampling theory is the percentage of errors, however errors are defined. This is a considerable limitation, but it does not destroy the usefulness of the method. It does require, however, that the profession give careful thought to the levels of errors which can be labeled acceptable or unacceptable. It would seem that any standard selected must be based upon small percentages for both hypotheses. This follows from general considerations of the nature of accounting work, in which a high degree of accuracy is clearly possible and is, in most cases, attained. Evidently some allowance for error should be made in the acceptable hypothesis, since errorless accounting is unknown and, furthermore, zero is not a workable basis for use of the formulas of sequential sampling. The values for the hypothetical populations which are here tentatively suggested are $p_1 = 0.005$ and $p_2 = 0.03$ (the values reflected in the first half of table 10), that is, that the acceptable population be defined as one with 0.5 per cent errors or fewer, and the unacceptable one as having 3 per cent errors or more. This means that a population with 1 error in 200 calculations or entries is definitely acceptable, and one with 3 errors in 100 is not. It has been noted that other possibilities may be selected; table 10 gives data on $p_1 = 0.005$ and $p_2 = 0.05$; table 12 gives certain characteristics of different values for p_1 and p_2. It may be noted at this point that the quantity of sampling which is required depends to a high degree, in the sequential method, upon the size of the gap between the hypotheses. This can be seen on a common-sense basis in the fact that, as the values of p_1 and p_2 are separated more and more, the samples likely to be drawn from either population become more and more different and hence indicate the conclusion for an actual case more and more quickly.

It may be appropriate to apply a less rigorous standard for the ratio of errors to those areas of the accounting where the possibility or cost of accuracy does not permit so high a standard as applies generally. This procedure seems most justified in the physical count of inventory. Here access to the stock may be difficult, personnel is under heavy pressure, and a multitude of conditions may conspire to create many small discrepancies. In any ruditing situation the nature of the errors found and the magnitude of errors possible have a bearing on any decision about the adequacy of the accounts and provide sufficient safeguard so that, if a rigorous definition of error is used, it may be appropriate to set a lower standard for conditions in which there is no economic possibility of maintaining the general standard. In other words, the percentage of errors is one index of quality, not its sole measure.

NATURE OF ERRORS TABULATED FOR STATISTICAL INTERPRETATION

A definition of error for use in applying the techniques discussed in the first two chapters is essential, since conditions describable by the term "error" are numerous in auditing.

Errors may be classed in two general groups—those which are substantive in financial statements and those which indicate only a breakdown of control without direct substantive effect. The latter will be referred to hereafter as "procedural" errors. The failure to record a liability would be a substantive error, and the failure to put a countersignature upon a check otherwise properly issued would represent only a breakdown of control or a procedural error. Substantive errors are: (1) errors in computations; (2) errors in posting; (3) errors in accounting principle; (4) omissions.

The first type of substantive error is illustrated by an error in an extension or footing; its nature is purely arithmetical. The nature of the second is mechanical—and evident. The third may be exemplified by the charging of repairs to a capital asset account—or, what is more probable, the charging of capital items to repairs. Omissions from the accounts are most likely to represent liabilities, adjustments for accruals or deferments, or sales, and in any of these cases to be concentrated at the closing date. It may be observed that this concentration will not interfere with the interpretation of samples on a statistical basis for the following reasons: the sampling presumably will be random, hence the closing entries will not be disproportionately represented; explicit attention is given to the closing entries to the extent that they will be examined in detail rather than by sample in most cases; and the closing entries will in most cases be relatively few so that they are not likely to form a satisfactory group or area of the accounting for a single application of statistical technique—as will the listing and computation of a sizable inventory, for example.

The breakdown of control at any point is defined as an error because much of the auditing is performed to investigate the functioning of the system of internal control, the adequacy of which is generally considered a major justification for the use of a sampling procedure. Tabulation as an error of any specific failure to conform to the rules of internal control in effect on the particular engagement will provide a measure of the effectiveness of that control which will be valid in spite of the fact that the individual case may not be substantive with respect to the statements, since some kind of breakdown in control is the means by which any error comes into existence, and we must consider the likelihood that there are no important substantive errors on the basis of the quality of control which is inferred from the sample.

In connection with procedural errors it must be stipulated that an error will consist of a violation of the rules actually in effect in the particular organization being audited, since a failure to use desirable methods of internal control cannot be given a numerical expression useful in statistical inference. This means that a decision will have to be made by the auditor using statistical methods, exactly as is done at present, on whether the rules of internal check supposed to be in effect are adequate *if followed* to give a satisfactory accounting; it means, too, that the statistical procedure will be useful in determining whether the actual *functioning* of the process is satisfactory. In view of the many limitations upon the use of internal check in the very diverse organizations which customarily issue certified statements, of the human element involved, and of the fact that existence of control is not a matter of rules but of results in any accounting process, the test of the functioning of the system is certainly the most important part of the process of examination.

The present author concludes that all substantive and procedural errors should be tabulated for purposes of statistical interpretation. Only by such inclusiveness can a complete measure (on a binomial basis) be obtained of the conditions surrounding the accounts. It is also desirable that the methods used provide as large a number of errors as a reasonable definition can make possible, since reasonably accurate accounting will show a very small ratio of errors in any case and a sufficient number for purposes of observation is essential to any mathematical treatment of them.

THE DISCOVERY OF FRAUD THROUGH STATISTICAL INFERENCE

Obviously, the errors encountered may be deliberate, made either for purposes of putting a more favorable aspect upon the accounts for credit, tax, or similar purposes, or to conceal embezzlement. This possibility raises the question of the power of statistical methods to uncover fraud. There is only one advantage to be gained from the use of statistical inference in the disclosure of fraud: by establishing an objective basis for the acceptance of the conclusion that adequate control exists in a set of accounts, including a minimum sample size, auditors may continue to examine particular cases beyond the point at which they would stop if the decision rested upon subjective judgment alone, and so they may be led to disclosures which otherwise would remain unopened. In other words, an auditor could not, if using a statistical standard for the percentage of errors acceptable, conclude after examining a conventional proportion of the entries (in which he found numerous mistakes which appeared insignificant individually and offsetting in effect) that the accounts, though "sloppy," were acceptable. If an unqualified certificate were to be issued, it would be necessary to continue examining the entries as long as a higher-than-standard ratio of errors was indicated. In this extended process falsifications might be uncovered which would not otherwise be found.

The possibility discussed above is not of great weight in a decision to use statistical methods, since no sampling procedure can with a high degree of certainty be directed toward the discovery of fraud. Such an investigation must be undertaken by a very close review of all individual transactions in the area suspected of concealing fraud. This view is well known among professional accountants, who are particularly careful to avoid the impression that the ordinary audit is so designed as to justify the expectation that occasional frauds will be discovered.

The discovery of fraud, furthermore, rests upon the ability of the auditor to recognize its presence by consideration of the nature and implications of the error; it will not appear as a conclusion from the fact that an error exists. Statistical inference will not increase the ability of the auditor to recognize fraud, and it must be undertaken, as the sampling process is undertaken at present, upon the assumption that fraud is not present. It will be helpful in this direction only where it prevents a too-ready acceptance of accounts in which a generally low level of performance is accompanied by deliberate falsification.

APPLICATIONS OF STATISTICAL INFERENCE TO SPECIFIC ACCOUNTS, RECORDS, AND COMPUTATIONS

INVENTORY

The physical inventory is an especially appropriate place for the application of statistical methods of auditing. It is commonly composed of numerous items of stock, most of which are small relative to the total value. It cannot, therefore, ordinarily be counted or measured in its entirety by the auditor. Under the *Extensions of Auditing Procedure*[2] enunciated by the American Institute of Accountants in 1939 the auditor is required, wherever he represents himself as having used "generally accepted auditing procedure," "wherever practicable and reasonable" to "be present . . . at the inventory-taking and by suitable observation and inquiry satisfy himself as to the effectiveness of the methods of inventory-taking and as to the measure of reliance which may be placed upon the client's representations as to inventories and upon the records thereof. In this connection the independent certified public accountant may require physical tests of inventories to be made under his observation." Although emphasis is placed upon the client's responsibility for the representation and upon the degree of *control* in effect, and actual count or measurement by the auditor is not made mandatory,[3] it is nonetheless the chief or at least a very prominent part of the process as it is applied in practice. From his own count of some of the items, his general view of the rules for control of the process, and his observation of their use, the auditor will proceed from the assumption of a satisfactory condition and its successful meeting of the challenge of the sample to the conclusion of acceptability. This is the process which has been described in general terms in previous pages of this work.

The errors to be tabulated in physical inventory include errors in counting the quantities, errors in identifying the stock, wrong prices, errors in grading, and in the clerical work of extensions and footings. If the inventory is voluminous, each of these processes may be taken as a separate area of the accounting and sampled for the purpose of testing the quality of the control in that particular area.

[2] American Institute of Accountants, New York, October, 1939.

[3] The bulletin of the same title issued May 9, 1939, was less equivocal on this point. It includes the following statements: "Your committee believes that corroboration of inventory quantities by physical tests should be accepted as normal audit procedure" (p. 3), and ". . . also, he shall wherever practicable and reasonable make, or where the inventory taking is adequately planned and controlled observe the making of, physical tests by count, weight or measurement, for the purpose of satisfying himself that the methods of inventory taking have been carried out effectively and for the purpose of testing the accuracy of recording of quantities in the inventory records; . . ." (p. 4).

If it is small, it will be necessary to tabulate all the types of error and to make an over-all interpretation. It is also possible, as has been suggested before, to divide the inventory by departments or locations and to test for control over such areas. Any division that is made should reflect different influences which determine the issue of accuracy, such as different personnel; the advantage in so dividing the material for the statistical tests lies in the possibility that poor work, if it exists, is present in some areas and not in others, so that additional samples may be taken only where the issue is in doubt. It is also appropriate to test for bias in the direction of error in the inventory; note should be taken of the fact that any willful effort to manipulate inventory values may be spread through the several processes of calculation, so the test is preferably applied to the errors on an over-all basis. This consideration is further supported by the fact that errors which are biased in direction by chance alone will not be restricted to any segment of the work. Naturally, procedural errors, such as failure to sign an inventory sheet as required for fixing responsibility in the counting, will not be included in the latter test. Sample size will be calculated as indicated previously, consideration being given to the minimum sample required to permit an acceptance on the probability level and hypothetical ratios of errors adopted.

Where the auditor is not present for the physical inventory taking, he may make independent counts of the stock at the time of his visit. This procedure will be designed to corroborate the quantities, to which he may then apply the statistical technique. For the pricing and other elements of the work the company's records will be used as in other cases. It will be necessary, of course, to reconcile the independent count with the reported stocks.

In perpetual inventory records, two aspects require attention: the physical confirmation of the book record, and the clerical adequacy of the record independent of physical check. Where physical inventories are taken at various times during the year, the auditor may apply the same technique as in a year-end physical inventory, except that he will probably not be able to be present for the physical testing of as many items as in the other case. In such a case the minimum sample as calculated from statistical considerations will be important, and special consideration should be given to the randomness of the physical test.

Clerical accuracy of the book record, which is relied upon for the inventory figure in the absence of a physical inventory at the closing date, will be tested by the auditor through reference to receiving records and stores requisitions or shipping documents and by checking extensions, postings, and footings. Errors noted in these records and computations may be tabulated and interpreted as in other clerical work. Two of the cases given at the end of this chapter deal with inventory. The cases will illustrate, and to some extent confirm, the validity of statistical method in auditing.

ACCOUNTS RECEIVABLE

Emphasis in the examination of accounts receivable is placed at present upon confirmation by correspondence. It is universally concluded that correspondence with every customer who has an open balance at a particular closing date is not necessary, but the number of accounts which should be so examined in any case is indefinite under current practice. The position taken by accountants generally is expressed in the *Extensions of Auditing Procedure* (October, 1939) by the recommendation that "the method, extent, and time of confirming receivables in each engagement, and whether of all receivables or a part thereof, be determined by the independent certified public accountant as in other phases of procedure requiring the exercise of his judgment." In contrast with the foregoing, we may recall that it is possible to set an absolute minimum number of accounts to be circularized in order to come to a decision on the selected probability level, and that standards may be specified which require larger samples and which substitute objective probability for individual judgment.

The errors to be tabulated for statistical interpretation in connection with correspondence upon accounts (and notes) receivable should include all points of difference between the client and his customer except discrepancies in the date of entry by the two parties that reflect only a normal interval. Any unreasonable delay in the recording by one party should, of course, be investigated, since it may be indicative of lack of agreement on proper dating of a charge or application of a credit, either of these conditions being substantive in that the amount or valuation of the receivables may be affected.

When a reply confirming the record is requested from the customer, as contrasted with the request for information only when the customer disagrees with the record, the question arises of the significance of the cases in which no response is received. In the absence of any specific reason to suspect such cases (a suspicion which might be based, e.g., on the fact that they were disproportionate in number to previous experience) the usual conclusion of practice must be adopted; namely, that replies were not received because the customer had no exception to make. This may not always be true, since the reply may be neglected through carelessness or because it involves appreciable work on the part of the customer's staff—as in those cases where accounts payable are not kept in ledger form but are handled through a voucher system—but it nevertheless seems to be the only workable assumption. The foregoing discussion accordingly suggests that the size of the sample will be determined from the number of requests mailed and not from the number of replies received since failure to receive a reply is taken as acceptance of the record. This does not preclude a second request when more positive assurance is desired.

The above paragraphs have dealt with accounts receivable in terms of account balances. In some cases it may be necessary to rely upon an examination of original records for purposes of verifying the accounts; this is generally true of accounts with government bodies, which, as a matter of legal policy, usually refuse to sign confirmation requests. Here the tabulation of errors will include any substantive or procedural error encountered in the area selected for testing. This area may be taken to include all the original records and journals primarily or largely concerned with accounts receivable—that is, those relating to sales and cash receipts—or the separate journals with their supporting papers may be taken as independent areas for testing. The first method will be convenient when the testing is centered around the accounts receivable, as when the entries in several accounts are traced back to original records and some original records traced through to the accounts as one integrated operation, and the second method will be appropriate where the work is organized around the journals, each journal being examined in turn and the postings tested to give an adequate verification of the resulting ledger accounts.

Where accounts receivable ledgers are divided and the division is followed in interpreting samples by drawing separate samples from the several divisions, the test for accounting control over the group may be invoked to decide the question whether or not one which shows too many errors for acceptance as an isolated case can be accepted upon the showing of all the samples. Where substantive errors run more in one direction than the other, the test for bias in the direction of error may be applied.

BOOKS OF ORIGINAL ENTRY AND RELATED RECORDS

1. Checks.—It is customary to scrutinize a selected number of bank checks for proper signature, dating, indorsement, and entry, the last consisting of a comparison of amount, date, and payee as disclosed on the checks with the respective entries in the cash disbursements journal. This process is usually followed by a test of the footings and postings of the journal for the period in which the selected checks are entered. Although the bulletin of the American Institute of Accountants, *Examination of Financial Statements,*[4] outlines as generally accepted auditing procedure one requiring no more examination of checks than is necessary to ascertain that the bank reconciliation is in order, it is common practice to examine checks in some month other than the closing month in order to test the internal control over cash disbursements. When the latter operation

---

[4] American Institute of Accountants, New York, January, 1936. Although this bulletin is the most recent one to give very specific auditing procedures, it is to some degree obsolete at the present time.

is undertaken, statistical methods are obviously appropriate. It may be noted in passing that the randomness of the sample becomes important at this point, since the test is presumed to apply to the whole period under audit, whereas the usual practice is to examine the checks recorded in one month. This subject will be considered specifically in chapter v and is accordingly deferred for the present. It is also evident that errors to be tabulated for statistical inferences in the accounting for checks include the points of scrutiny mentioned in the preceding paragraph plus a memorandum of any missing checks, which may be noted from the journals or, in cases where forms are prenumbered, from the continuity of check numbers. As before, the existence of a rule of internal check upon any point will determine whether any specific instance of inadequate control can be tabulated for statistical treatment or whether it must be separately considered in the decision to apply a sampling technique.

2. Cash disbursement vouchers.—Here again an examination is typically made for a selected time within the period under review as a check upon the validity of disbursements and of their recording. For this purpose a voucher document, including the supplier's invoice, the client's receiving report, and other original records is usually available; when this document is not available separate reference must be made to the original records which are significant in the substantiation of the transaction, but the tabulation of errors may proceed in the same way as when the combination of forms in one voucher is used.

The auditor will examine vouchers for certain well-known points; genuineness of documents, propriety of purchase, receipt of goods, changed dates, raised amounts, proper approval, and proper journal entry. It will be noted that much of the effort in determining the foregoing points seems to refer essentially to a precaution against fraud. This is more apparent than real, since public accountants generally do not conduct the typical balance sheet audit so as to be reasonably certain of discovering any fraud which may exist. The method is to examine those parts of the accounts essential to a confirmation of the balance sheet at a certain date, to supplement this with review and examination of the detail of the accounts sufficient to give the auditor assurance that the balances emerge from an adequately conducted accounting and may thus be audited without the complete verification that would be required if no reliance could be placed upon the internal control. Where a statement of profit and loss is presented, as is now the typical case, the vouching must be undertaken in order to test the propriety of the classification of expenses. The errors that the auditor will expect to find in the ordinary instance will therefore be errors in computation, in classification within the accounts, and procedural errors, such as failure to obtain the approval of the proper executive in the form of his signature or initials on the voucher document.

All those exceptions to the vouchers which the auditor will regularly take as he examines them, even though the error be corrected before the audit is completed (as in cases where a required signature is obtained) will contribute to the tabulation of errors for statistical interpretation, since they are the measure of quality which existed in the material presented to the auditor. The size of the sample to be examined may be computed as before; when the vouchers for a month have customarily been examined, it will be found, in all but distinctly small concerns, that the minimum sample required by the statistical method is smaller than the number of vouchers usually examined. However, the question of sample size will be more important if random sampling is adopted, since the latter is characteristically more time-consuming per voucher than the examination of a series of contiguous vouchers. The method of filing vouchers used by the client is also a consideration.

In large concerns there may be enough substantive errors in the sample to justify application of the test for bias in the direction of error.

3. Pay rolls.—Pay rolls form an integrated area of the cash disbursements and accordingly are separately handled in the constructive accounting process and in the auditing. They are analogous to inventories in that they constitute a record built up entirely within the client's organization, though the scrutiny applied by the individual worker to his check is somewhat equivalent to an outside scrutiny of the record. Since the only source of data and all computations are entirely an internal product of the client's organization, pay rolls receive special attention in the review of internal control.

Pay-roll errors may arise at several points: in the recording or transcribing of time worked or units of goods produced; in the calculation of earnings and deductions; and in the preparation of the pay roll and checks. It is customary in the typical audit to test this record by reference to some of the time cards (often those for a week chosen at random) which are then traced through the successive stages of pay-roll preparation into the pay-roll book. The latter will then ordinarily be compared with the pay-roll checks for a week or month, its footings tested, and the postings traced into the ledgers. This process lends itself as well as those previously described to statistical methods of testing. In concerns with a very large pay roll and when a considerable amount of detailed verification of pay roll is undertaken, it may be appropriate to divide the application of the statistical procedure and to consider each step in the process, as outlined in the first sentence of this paragraph, as a separate area of the accounts. This procedure is reasonable since the processes will be under somewhat differing control in a large organization where the work is necessarily divided. For most audits, however, the whole process of pay-roll preparation and payment can best be taken as one area and all errors noted in it tabulated for one test of probability.

Sample size may be determined as before. Since pay-roll errors that penalize the worker are more likely to be disclosed and corrected than those that overstate the amount due the worker, the test for bias in the direction of error may be especially fruitful in applications to large pay rolls.

4. Petty cash vouchers.—These items may be treated, as are other cash disbursement vouchers, as a part of the audit of the cash disbursements generally, but one element of special interest arises: petty cash is less easily controlled and less easily vouched than are general cash disbursements, and it is often given particular attention by the auditor on this account. It will therefore form a separate area for statistical purposes wherever the volume of petty cash vouchers is large.

It is characteristic of petty cash vouchers that they are less likely to be complete than are the vouchers which support bank disbursements. This is because the transactions in petty cash are conducted more informally than others, so that documents are not always readily available and individual forgetfulness has unusual opportunity to operate. It will frequently be found that receipts for postage are missing, for example. Where definite rules are established requiring the preparation of vouchers to support petty cash disbursements, however, deviations from them must be tabulated as errors if an objective measure of the control in effect is to be secured. Fortunately, petty cash transactions are usually few enough so that the auditor can examine all of them where the control is poor, in which case the total amount of inadequately supported transactions may be determined and appropriate action taken.

5. Cash receipts.—The examination of cash receipts is undertaken, as in other cases where detail is examined, generally for the purpose of ascertaining that the handling of receipts is proper. Attention will be given to certain elements of the cash receipts record solely for the purpose of verifying the closing balance, such as the inquiry into the possibility that the books were held open after the closing date or that a check was "kited" to provide a last-minute deposit. Where, however, deposits for months other than the closing one are checked against bank statements, where details of deposit slips at interim dates are compared with details in the cash receipts book, and where, both in interim periods and in the final month, footings in and postings from the cash receipts journal are checked, the procedure is designed to test the entire cash receipts accounting process for the period and it may appropriately be carried out with the aid of statistical method.

Aside from the possibility of fraud, the errors in cash receipts are likely to be minor, and, as noted before, statistical inference will be of little benefit in looking for fraud. The relative infrequency of errors of a mechanical or procedural sort in the cash receipts is due to two facts: the receipts are checked by outside contacts at two points, the remitter and, usually, the bank of deposit; and they are characteristically handled with a minimum of documentation. An error in the amount of credit to a customer's account brings an inquiry from him; an error in transcribing the amount of a check in the journal and on the deposit slip brings a correction from the bank. It is rare for a concern to prepare a slip to record the details of a remittance; it is almost universal that the amount is entered in the cash receipts book from a check. Where currency is received regularly in a wholesale business, receipt forms will usually be available, but this is an exceptional situation; in retailing the common arrangement for the recording of currency receipts is the cash register. Since the customer's check is deposited and is then returned by the bank to the customer, the auditor must usually begin with the cash receipts journal and deposit slips in examining receipts of a wholesale concern and with cash register tapes in a retail concern. This practice leaves comparatively little scope for a tabulation of errors suitable to testing control over cash receipts, and explains why much of the auditing procedure in this area is directed toward the discovery of fraud or more or less willful manipulation of the accounts. The practice of comparing details of deposits according to the cash journal with copies of deposit slips obtained from the bank, for example, is applicable chiefly as a safeguard against "lapping," and the investigation of the "cutoff" is chiefly concerned with the "window-dressing" possible through a reduction of accounts receivable and an increase in cash on the balance sheet and with other fraudulent devices. Some opportunity to make a statistical test remains in the checking of the footings and postings of the cash receipts book, and it occasionally arises at other points; for example, when cash register tapes or receipt forms are available. Receipt forms are available when collectors are employed for house-to-house work, for example. The method is therefore recommended for cash receipts, though it is thought that it will not be so fruitful here as in some other sections of the accounts.

Statistical methods of the kind advocated in the present work will not aid in determining what cash should have been received; indeed, auditors generally refuse to take responsibility for ascertaining this fact in any ordinary audit, and will do so only where they are retained to make a detailed investigation. Rough calculations based upon gross profits rates are frequently made; where inventory records are adequate the stock handled may be reconciled roughly with cash received, or at least the stock record will be examined for evidence that all goods purchased or produced are accounted for, thus indicating that all sales are recorded. Such investigations must be undertaken in some detail, and no statistical hypotheses can be constructed which have generality enough to substitute economically for direct verification in each case.

6. *Sales.*—Some examination of sales invoices and shipping records, together with the sales journal, is regularly undertaken as a test of the control over the recording of sales revenue. The extent of the test is usually very limited, a week's transactions in the usual case being about the maximum, and it is commonly coupled with the examination of the "cutoff," so that only transactions at the end of the fiscal period come into view. The original records related to sales—invoices, shipping orders, and customers' orders (when available), with, of course, the sales journal—are clearly a proper area of the accounting for application of statistical method. The substantive errors discoverable in this process will consist largely of clerical errors in the recording of invoices in the journal and in the footing and posting of the journal, and, occasionally, of instances in which goods shipped do not correspond with the invoice. In the latter case the error is likely to run against the client, for obvious reasons. When a check of extensions on invoices is made by the auditor, this will provide another source for exceptions.

Since the customer acts as an influence tending to accuracy in the record of sales, it is to be expected that fewer errors of a substantive type will be disclosed in this area than in some other sections of the accounts. There is, nevertheless, more than sufficient justification for a check upon the quality of control over sales in the possibilities that an invoice may not be issued for a shipment, that more goods may be shipped than invoiced, and that clerical errors of computation and posting or of omission of a transaction from the journal may arise. Where a test for bias in the direction of error indicates a disproportionate number of cases in which sales revenue has been improperly recorded, with the result that the client received less than should have been obtained for his goods, it may be necessary to qualify the certificate to the effect that "sufficient examination has not been made to satisfy the auditor that the methods of recording sales revenue are adequate." Procedural errors in sales will assist to measure the quality of control. Examples of such errors are: failure of the shipping department to stamp on a shipping order the date of shipment, or failure of the credit department representative to initial a customer's order to indicate his approval of the extension of credit.

7. *Ledger footings and postings.*—This item may become a distinct area for examination of the accounts—as distinguished from cases in which footings and postings of accounts are checked incidental to the testing of a particular book of original entry—when the check of clerical accuracy in the keeping of the general ledger is undertaken as a distinct function in the audit. This is done where the ledger contains a considerable number of accounts not analyzed in the course of the audit and hence subject to clerical errors which might go unobserved without this procedure. It may also be undertaken as a division of the work relative to any other ledger, as accounts receivable or factory ledger. The errors discoverable will be errors of account selection in posting, a very few offsetting arithmetical errors, and, of course, willful errors if present. The latter will receive attention far beyond statistical method, and the offsetting errors will be rare; other arithmetical errors in ledger posting and footing will be discovered in taking trial balances. Posting to the wrong account remains the chief object of statistical attention in this area; where the volume of postings is large it is a proper object for application of the statistical method.

CAPITAL AND MAINTENANCE EXPENDITURES

The distinction between capital and maintenance, or revenue, expenditures is a crucial one for the calculation of periodic income and the statement of assets at any date. It receives proportionate attention in auditing. In concerns where capital additions are few, the capital accounts will be analyzed and vouched completely for the period under review. In many cases, however, the volume of additions to capital is so large as to render a complete vouching, or, on occasion, complete analysis, uneconomical, and this is usually true of maintenance charges. Under these circumstances the practice is to analyze and vouch all capital additions over a selected amount in cost, and to vouch a sample of the others, and to follow a similar practice in repairs. The classification or stratification of the data may be incorporated in the sampling procedure with an improvement in the sample as a result. This process will be described in chapter v. The individual amounts appearing in the journals are the basis for the selection of the items to be checked in full and those to be sampled, as distinguished from a physical unit, such as a machine.

Where a sampling procedure is adopted, it is desirable to use objective statistical methods, and in the present instance it is possible to set the number of items to be sampled (at minimum or otherwise) and to decide without subjective fallibility whether the additions to capital assets or the charges to maintenance can be accepted without further sampling. The error with which we are concerned here is the question of whether an item has been charged to the proper category—capital or maintenance. This is simple statistically, but requires nice decisions in practice on the nature of a particular item. Where the client uses some arbitrary rule for excluding small charges from capital asset accounts—for example, that no item costing less than fifty dollars shall be capitalized—it should be accepted for statistical purposes, though other action, such as disclosures in the accountant's report, may be required. Errors of a clerical nature surrounding the capital asset and maintenance accounts may be included in the process of statistical inference about them if desired, but they relate to a somewhat larger question of control than the single issue of proper classification of expenditures, and the latter is of sufficient importance to be independently tested.

CASE MATERIALS

The following case materials are presented as illustrations of the application of statistical methods to auditing procedure, and they serve also to confirm what has been said here about the efficacy of those methods. The first three cases are actual case histories drawn from practice; the last one is hypothetical.

CASE I

Case I deals primarily with the merchandise inventory of a very large, limited-price, variety chain store. It is possible to use this inventory material as a check on statistical methods because of the processing it received in the head office of the client. Inventory books listing, pricing, and extending the stock were prepared at each store and then forwarded to the head office where they were put through a complete clerical process before acceptance for record. This process included the checking of all footings and extensions, and a review of each price by merchandise managers. A correction sheet was prepared for each book so that all errors were readily traced. We therefore have in the books as originally prepared a population typical of a large body of auditing situations, and from the auditing process we know with a high degree of certainty the actual quality of the work done on the inventory by the store's personnel. We can apply statistical procedures to the inventory as it was prepared by the stores, and compare results with what we know to be true of the stock as a result of the complete examination made of it afterward. Twenty-one stores and a total of 73,415 inventory items are involved in the tabulations which follow; errors of extension and footing are included; errors of footing are included in the sample simply by taking each footing as one of the items in the material examined and giving it a numerical position wherever it falls in the succession of items—thus, if there are twenty extensions to the page, the footing of page one is item number 21. It is, of course, possible to treat the footings as a separate area for testing, and this will be appropriate where different employees from those performing extension have done the footing. In the present case the employees were the same in the two cases.

For purposes of our trial of statistical methods in this case a random sample of 77 items[5] was drawn from the items in the inventory of each of the twenty-one stores, so that a conclusion could be drawn about the quality of the work done at each location. This is a larger sample for the whole group than was taken for purposes of the actual audit, where 25 items per store were tested for extension, and five pages in each book footed. A price test for 25 items was made from each of ten stores in the actual case; in terms of footings and extensions the actual audit included a test of 630 items, and the test applied here involves, 1,617. The larger test has been used as a more rigorous trial of the statistical method; each store is tested here as an individual case in applying statistical method, but it would have been perfectly appropriate to make one test of the inventory as a whole for actual auditing use. The saving in the extent of the test when it is placed upon an over-all basis is therefore the difference between 77 and 630 items, if we anticipate the findings which are discussed below. A single minimum sample of 77 and another of 175 were also drawn from the group as a whole. The drawing was made by use of random sampling numbers (chap. v), the position of the errors in the population being known.

The results of the sampling of each of the stores, together with the actual number of items and actual errors present, are shown in table 2.

As is to be expected in drawing samples of 77 from populations where the percentage of error is less than 3 per cent, and particu-

[5] This being the minimum number for acceptance under the values set up for the test as follows: $p_1 = 0.001$ (a more stringent value than the 0.005 of table 10), $p_2 = 0.03$, $a = 0.05$ and $\beta = 0.10$. As before p_1 defines the desirable population, p_2 defines the undesirable one, a is the risk of mistakenly rejecting a good population, and β is the risk of mistakenly accepting a bad one.

larly where it is very much less than that amount, errors turn up in the sample very rarely. Here the store with the highest percentage of error is number 11, which had 1.5 per cent errors; the percentages were too small, therefore, to enable us to expect to see one error in a sample of 77.

TABLE 2

STORE INVENTORY POPULATIONS AND ERRORS FOUND IN RANDOM SAMPLES OF 77

Store number	Number of items in store inventory (extensions and footings)	Actual number of errors present	Number of errors drawn in random sample of 77
1....................	5721	1	0
2....................	5303	3	0
3....................	3776	16	0
4....................	3837	7	0
5....................	3378	4	0
6....................	3719	6	1
7....................	4211	9	0
8....................	3693	19	0
9....................	2120	6	0
10....................	4050	5	0
11....................	2862	43	0
12....................	2647	6	0
13....................	3821	15	0
14....................	4278	14	0
15....................	3437	17	0
16....................	2161	2	0
17....................	2638	0	0
18....................	2580	5	0
19....................	2601	0	0
20....................	2330	9	0
21....................	4252	14	0
Totals............	73,415	201	1

In every store except number 6, where one error was found, we would have accepted the population as more likely to be 0.001 than 0.03 defective, since a sample of 77 with no errors included indicates acceptance on a sequential basis. This includes store 11 which actually has a percentage of error very slightly closer to 0.03 than to 0.001, so this store represents one of the infrequent cases which we contemplate when we set the risks. In store 6 where one error was found it is to be noted that this was the ninth item drawn for this store. Where $p_1 = 0.001$, $p_2 = 0.03$, $\alpha = 0.05$ and $\beta = 0.10$, rejection is called for if an error is found in the first 18 items taken. On the chance that the sample was unrepresentative, the normal auditing procedure would be to take more items for the sample. This was done for store 6 in the present case; it was necessary to take another 116 items, since the population could not be accepted as more likely to be 0.001 than 0.03 defective after one error had been found until 193 items were included in the sample. No more errors were found in the 116 additional items and the population, in actual practice, would have been accepted, as we know it should be.

In the samples of 77 and of 175 which were taken separately on an over-all basis, no errors were found. Since the 73,415 items included 201 errors, the actual ratio of defectives is 0.0027. In saying, therefore, that we accept 0.001 as a better estimate of this than 0.03 we would have reached the right conclusion on an over-all basis. In view of the saving of work which could be made in this case, the plea for statistical method should be clear.

Two other areas of the audit under consideration are of interest in sample size. The first of these is the audit of store alterations accounts, which represent fixed assets. All individual additions of more than $500 in those stores having total additions of $5,000 or more during the year were listed and vouched. Four of the twenty-one stores had more than $5,000 of additions; the items of $500 or more totaled 150. No errors were found in this group, and no smaller items were examined. It would have been appropriate here to take 77 of the items of $500 or more at random and to interpret them as indicative of all the items of $500 or more on the basis suggested for the inventory test. Although the exact character of the population of $500 items is not known in this case (since only those at stores with $5,000 of additions during the year were examined) it is extremely likely that few if any errors were present, and the interpretation of a sample of 77 with no errors would, of course, have given the same conclusion as the examination of the 150 actually did. In addition, the test would have been improved in generality.

This improvement could have been carried further to include the smaller items in a random sample without taking a larger sample than was needed for the more restricted test.

The other area of the case also deals with fixed assets: the account for fixtures. Here the record of balances of fixtures, maintained in the form of an annual inventory, was scrutinized for correspondence with the preceding year and additions or deductions vouched. Since the general ledger accounting is on an inventory basis, each item scrutinized is a part of the inventory and an item of the population, although the items representing additions and deductions are relatively more important. Counting all the items gives a population of 672; one error was found in the process of scrutiny and vouching when item 54 was scrutinized; a statistical sample of 193 would have been sufficient in this instance to give the correct conclusion, since only one error existed and when that turned up in the sample it meant only that enough items to permit acceptance with one error had to be drawn.

CASE II

The material of this case is the raw material and merchandise inventory of a small manufacturer of surgical appliances. The inventory consisted of 1,060 items, and the clerical work is the area tested. Extensive examination of this inventory in the actual audit, plus thorough scrutiny by the senior partner of the firm (who did not participate in its preparation) revealed only 5 errors. The examination of the clerical work was not complete, although 100 per cent of footings and 25 per cent of extensions were checked by the auditors. We may assume, however, that all errors were found for the purpose of trying statistical techniques. Upon such an assumption, three independent random samples were drawn from this inventory by means of the device used in Case I. In the first two samples no errors were found in the first 89 items drawn, so that the population would have been accepted with a minimum sample if we use the values of table 10 (left section) as a basis for judgment. In the third sample an error was found when item 45 was drawn;

this indicates an indeterminate result. A continuation of the drawing was made and after 160 items were included no other error had been found, so the population would have been accepted in the third case also without as much effort as was expended by the auditors in practice. In the event the reader is concerned about our failure to run down the 5 errors in this inventory, it should be observed at this point that where any error is considered likely to be very important and its discovery essential, the sampling method is not appropriate, whether applied scientifically or not. Such an attitude requires complete examination of the area involved.

CASE III

In view of the small number of errors in the populations of Cases I and II a case is needed for the sake of argument in which the percentage of errors is substantially more than 3 per cent. Case III represents the interline freight settlements (accounts payable) of a large interstate transportation company during four months of a recent year. This accounts payable material serves the purpose well because the settlement is initiated by other carriers who present statements, and detailed audit is required before acceptance of the statement as a basis for settlement; we can, therefore, determine whether the results from sampling the material as it is presented by other carriers leads to conclusions we know to be proper as a result of the complete audits. The material in hand does not cover all settlements of the paying company during the period in question; only settlements with certain lines were selected, and lines known to be inadequately staffed and prone to errors were selected in order to try the statistical techniques on populations heavily defective. The situation presented here is one more likely to be the concern of internal than external auditors, and is exactly the situation of accountants who carry on the process of checking the representations of suppliers, a process often described as a form of audit; it nevertheless may occasionally be met by the public accountant, and in any event will serve to show the power of sequential sampling procedure.

The process of sampling upon a sequential basis permits the appraisal of the sample at each step of the drawing; accordingly, table 3 gives the number of items drawn from the interline accounts payable in question at each point where an error was discovered. We can thus see at a glance (given a basis for judgment, such as table

TABLE 3

INTERLINE ACCOUNTS PAYABLE

(Population data and results obtained by sequential sampling procedure)

Errors noted	Number of items in sample at point error is noted					
	Sept.	Oct.	Nov.	Dec.	Four months	
					Sample 1	Sample 2
1st.................	7	6	9	3	8	1
2d.................	10	12	12	7	13	15
3d.................	11	29	52	16	17	40
4th.................	29	79	59	31	25	45
5th.................	31	92	76	51	27	52
6th.................	34	98	93	52	41	55
7th.................	47	..	95	55	42	58
8th.................	57	..	..	67	44	60
9th.................	64	..	..	74	66	61
10th.................	66	..	..	94	76	64
11th.................	67	..	..	..	82	70
12th.................	68	..	..	..	83	79
13th.................	72	..	..	..	100	85
14th.................	79	..	..	..	..	..
15th.................	84	..	..	..	..	..
Actual per cent of errors in population.............	15.5	6.6	10.4	11.5	10.9	10.9

10, appendix ii) what our action might be if we were confronted with the populations in question in an actual case. The actual percentages of error present in the population are given at the bottom of the table; all are unacceptable by our usual standards. The process was terminated for experimental purposes upon discovery of 15 errors, although it would have been terminated much earlier in actual practice, assuming that the auditor did not undertake a complete examination of the area himself in order to render an unqualified certificate.

Using table 10 with $p_2 = 0.03$ as a basis for decision, we may note that rejection of any or all the months would be recognized as most likely to be necessary after examination of from only 7 to 15 items, since 2 errors were turned up within that number of items in each case, and 2 errors in any sample less than 30 are unacceptable. Furthermore, very little additional sampling is required to confirm the result, since 3 errors are disclosed in each case within 52 items at the most, and rejection is called for again. Any auditor meeting such a population would thus be given early and (where he has a knowledge of the mathematical probabilities which the table gives) convincing notice of the need to have the accounts in such an area reworked before they could be accepted. Where the errors are as frequent as in this case the amounts of misstatement involved are likely to be significant and in cash transactions with third parties the amounts recoverable are likely to repay the effort of intensive investigation.

The conclusion again is that the methods of interpretation of samples presented in this work are appropriate to and useful in auditing.

CASE IV

Since we cannot choose the percentage of error in an actual case, and in order to give the experimental material somewhat more generality, a hypothetical case providing populations with a variety of percentages of errors is presented. Here the population is 10,000 items in each instance, but various percentages of the items were designated as errors for the different samples as indicated in table 4. The use of populations of 1 per cent and 2 per cent defective without populations near to zero in defectives may give a biased impression of the effect of statistical methods, but it will emphasize the point that populations falling far inside the range of the two hypotheses require the greatest amount of sampling for a decision. The items which were to be taken as errors were identified by means of random numbers, and the samples were drawn by use of other random numbers. Two populations of 1 per cent defective are included; the results appear in table 4.

In no case was a 1 per cent population rejected, although in the first 1 per cent population a rather large sample had to be taken before a decision could be reached; acceptance is appropriate in this situation in view of the fact that 0.001 is a better estimate of a 1 per cent population than 0.03 is. A similarly satisfactory conclu-

TABLE 4

HYPOTHETICAL POPULATION OF 10,000 AND RESULTS OF SAMPLING

Number in sample	Number of defective items observed						
100..............................	2	0	1	3	5	10	21
130..............................	3	0	4	5	9	18	30
175..............................	2	2	2	4	9	17	43
290..............................	3	2	10	11	12	29	66
455..............................	5	5	12	15	21	46	109
Percentage of population defective....................	1	1	2	3	5	10	25

INTERPRETATION FROM TABLE 10
(where $P_2 = 0.03$)*

100..............................	i	a	i	r	r	r	r
130..............................	i	a	r	r	r	r	r
175..............................	i	i	i	i	r	r	r
290..............................	i	a	r	r	r	r	r
465..............................	a	a	r	r	r	r	r

* Substitute for number of defective items the symbols: a (accept); r (reject); i (indeterminate)

sion appears for the samples from the 2 per cent population; here we would expect the population to be rejected as more nearly 3 per cent than 0.1 per cent, and our samples call for rejection in 3 instances and give an indeterminate result in 2 others. It is significant that the samples of the populations with large percentages of error indicate rejection. Except for one sample (of 175) from the 3 per cent population which indicated no decision was yet possible, all the samples of this and of more defective populations call for rejection. Under these circumstances it appears that in none of these populations of 3 per cent or more defective would a wrong decision have been reached by the auditor, although we are prepared to find some such results. Many of the decisions involved in these samples would have been possible on a sequential basis long before the samples reached the sizes given (as can be more clearly seen from table 3), but the larger samples have been tabulated for the present case to indicate something of the effect of increasing sample sizes.

CHAPTER IV

A Statistical Basis for Auditing Standards and Costs

AUDITING STANDARDS

PURPOSES AND USERS

A STANDARD is a measuring device. In auditing, standards enable three groups of users to measure auditing performances with a reasonable degree of objectivity. First, they are desired to permit public agencies to judge the adequacy of specific auditing work. The interest of the Securities and Exchange Commission is most prominent in this connection in the United States, but other prospective and present users are found in the courts and in the state boards of accountancy. The latter group, being charged in many of the statutes with maintaining rules of professional conduct, must set up standards, but they have made no such progress as has the S. E. C. in enforcing standards designed to distinguish between a *bona fide* but inadequate audit and one of accepted quality. Indeed, it is the common experience of state boards of accountancy that courts will not uphold their efforts to revoke a license unless a felony is proved against the licensee. The establishment of unequivocal standards through their nearly universal acceptance by the public accounting profession would pave the way for effective maintenance of a high level of practice by the state boards.

The second group of users of auditing standards are students and young or new practitioners. The present writer has frequently found that students express frustration at the lack of objective standards in auditing, especially with respect to the size of sample, or, to use the professional term, the extent of the test. The question of how much to test has also been put to the author by persons beginning practice, and, of course, it is often discussed by practitioners of all degrees of experience. Where there is no guidepost of general validity to instruct the beginner, it is clearly too much to expect that he will develop a judgment which can consistently be relied upon to correspond with the conclusions of other practitioners who have arrived at their position by a similarly indefinite process, or that all differences will be justifiable.

The third group of users of a professional standard comprises the established practitioners. For them it is an assurance of compliance with the fundamental requirements of their work and a basis for resisting improper suggestions of curtailing the work; it constitutes, in the use of statistical inference based upon rigorous mathematics, an effective means of determining what is actually required in the way of data to permit an intelligent and defensible decision. Without this process of reasoning, the usual solution has been for each person or firm to develop a pattern or policy which governs his or its own choice of samples, the pattern being rather freely variable to meet changing circumstances, including, it is to be feared, ill-advised demands for economy. The situation would have to be tolerated if it were unavoidable, as practitioners have believed up to the present time. The calculation of the probability of drawing a particular sample from an acceptable population, and the procedures of inference derived from it, have, however, destroyed the validity of such a view. With this device, for the first time, a measure can be made of the adequacy of the *quantity* of work done in those parts of an audit where a sampling procedure is followed. Thus new entrants and old hands alike can determine what a minimum sample should be, given a probability level and acceptable hypothetical populations. So far as the courts and administrative bodies are concerned with the quantity of testing required, they too can rely upon statistical standards as soon as probability levels and standard percentages of allowable error are adopted.

In another sense every reader of a certified statement is a user of auditing standards, since he must rely upon the adequacy of the audit as his assurance of the fairness of the statement. The reader cannot be sure of the adequacy of a statement which was made up after inadequate sampling of the evidence which supposedly supports it, but he is not in the position of the other groups enumerated above and so cannot undertake specific criticism of the auditing procedures. This must be done by the profession and by regulating bodies. Appendix iii gives a brief history of the development of auditing standards in the United States.

STATISTICAL INFERENCE IN AUDITING STANDARDS

A major deterrent to the general acceptance of the movement toward the establishment of auditing standards has been that there has been no means for determining the extent of test or size of sample required to be taken, at least so far as its possession by auditors is concerned. Consequently, the feeling that any specification of procedure was certain to be arbitrary was inevitable. The mathematical reasoning available to the profession in statistical inference removes this stumbling block.

As has been noted previously, the statistical method provides a measure of the adequacy of the extent of test, and is the only objective measure of the quantity of work done in an audit. It applies only to the sampling part of the work, of course. Regardless of the controversy over standards versus procedures, it would seem that statistical inference should be a fundamental part of auditing standards. In distinguishing standards and procedures, the Committee on Auditing Procedures defines auditing standards as follows: "Auditing standards may be regarded as the underlying principles of auditing which control the nature and extent of the evidence to be obtained by auditing procedures."[1] No more fundamental principle is known for determining the extent of testing than that based on the mathematical probability of finding an error in a population where errors are present in objectionable numbers. Statistical inference qualifies, under the definition quoted, as a chief claimant to a place in auditing standards.

---

[1] *The Revised S.E.C. Rule on "Accountants Certificates,"* Statement on Auditing Procedure No. 6, Committee on Auditing Procedure, American Institute of Accountants, New York, March, 1941.

It must not be supposed that the adoption of a standard hypothesis for testing (i.e., for example, that the population has not more than 3 per cent of defectives) and a probability level (say 0.90) puts the auditor in a strait jacket by automatically finding his sample for him. In the first place, he must determine the area of the accounts which is to be judged by one sample, and this requires the exercise of professional judgment and skill that only a well-trained account- ant can muster. Second, the use of statistical inference requires a level of training which has never yet been considered anything short of professional. Last, the process is not over when the size of sample is determined, since the auditor must interpret the results and decide upon consequent action. Drawing the sample is also a field for pro- fessional skill, which the next chapter will discuss.

It need not be assumed that a single minimum sample is the only possible standard specification which can be made. In discussing standards in auditing, Samuel J. Broad[2] has pointed out clearly the importance of a matter which every competent auditor has in mind; namely, the need to consider the degree of risk attached to, and the materiality of, the items being verified when determining the amount and nature of the work to be done. It would be appropriate therefore to specify the mathematical probability basis differently for different areas of the accounts and degrees of materiality in the statements. This result could take the form in sequential sampling of specifying different values for p_1, p_2, α, and β for different areas of the accounts or different circumstances of the client. An example of an account immediately apparent as a candidate for special treatment is inven- tory, which is usually a very material item in the balance sheet and is always subject to miscalculations to a degree beyond that of the majority of accounts.

CONTENT OF A STATISTICAL STANDARD FOR AUDITING TESTS

1.Specification of the hypotheses on the population to be used.—As indicated in chapter i, any auditing sample may be appropriately interpreted upon the basis of two hypotheses linked by the likelihood

---

[2] "Auditing Standards," *Journal of Accountancy,* LXXII (Nov., 1941), 390–397.

ratio. In view of the fewness of errors, either procedural or substantive, which experience indicates as existing in the records of well-managed accounting departments, the present writer suggests a standard hypothesis of 3 per cent for the alternative estimate of the population from which the sample comes, and 0.5 per cent for the primary hypothesis. The profession may prefer to set other levels as experience is accumulated; it may be appropriate, where the objective of the sampling is conceived as a direct test of the content of the accounting statements, to set different levels for the acceptance or rejection of accounts from those used when the objective is instead a general test of the operation of the system of internal check and control. The reason for the difference is that it may be desirable to restrict the definition of error to substantive errors of significant (or specified) size in the former case, so that relatively few errors may be encountered as contrasted with the situation where all procedural errors are tabulated.

The specific values for the hypotheses suggested here are offered by the writer because he believes them to result in sample sizes which are reasonable for auditing use and because he feels that a larger proportion of errors than 3 per cent would indicate a degree of incompetence which would preclude acceptance of the accounts without very extensive checking.

2. Specification of the probability levels.—It is necessary that samples be taken which are adequate to reach decisions in most auditing cases without undue expense. This means that a few rare instances will arise in which a sample taken upon the basis of the standard procedure will fail to disclose an unsatisfactory condition or result in rejection of a satisfactory one. The frequency of such results is determined by the probability levels upon which the sample is interpreted—the α and β of the formulas. The values suggested here are 0.05 for α and 0.10 for β, such values being frequently used in general statistical practice.[8] Here again the levels are recommended because the writer feels they are consistent both with economy in auditing and with the risks which auditors may reasonably

---

[8] See appendix ii for further discussion of the symbols and formulas.

take. In this respect, the reader is reminded of the observations earlier on the fact that the drawing of a rare sample in a particular instance with the consequent wrong decision is by no means the equivalent of a failure in the whole audit, but is an error of much less amplitude. It should also be noted that making the risks objective does not increase them; many auditors may have been taking greater risks where no statistical inference was used.

AUDITING COSTS

COST OF THE SPECIFIC AUDIT

It was noted earlier in this work that interpretation of a sample drawn from a binomial population depended upon the absolute size of the sample and not upon the percentage relationship between the sample and the population.' The size of the sample may therefore be determined in advance without reference to the size of the population. This means that accountants may plan audit programs and estimate cost much more confidently than heretofore, since the use of samples determined as a given percentage of the entries subject to examination has been a very common if not characteristic device. The estimate of cost per item examined must be made as before, and in using statistical procedures it will be necessary to give consideration to the method of drawing the sample, which is the subject of the next chapter.

In the event that an unsatisfactory condition is indicated by the sample and further sampling is required if an unqualified certificate is to be given, the cost would, of course, be increased. This contingency should be provided for in the agreement with the client.

Clients have frequently been particularly concerned about special areas of the accounts, and the amount of testing in those areas has accordingly been increased in each case to suit the needs of the individual case. In the past the amount of work in such instances was

---

' This is not to say that large samples are not better; other things being equal, a larger sample is always better than a smaller one. It is also true that as a sample gets very large relative to the population, it becomes a better representation of the population as the sample size is increased.

arrived at subjectively; with statistical methods it is possible to stipulate that testing be carried on, once a minimum sample is taken, until interpretation of the findings upon a specified probability level indicates that the population is satisfactory.

Another situation in which the cost of auditing is a serious issue is that of the municipal audit. It has been the custom for municipalities to advertise for bids for their audits as for purchases of materials. The profession has protested the practice strongly, pointing out that the amount of work required can be determined accurately only as the examination proceeds, and contending that a fixed fee penalizes either the accountant or the municipality by providing more or less than is actually required to do the job, assuming that the accountant does not tailor the work to fit the fee, which he is obviously under pressure to do. The profession has urged a per diem rate for work actually required. Under these circumstances the specification that random tests of the transactions in particular areas of the municipal accounts shall be made and continued until interpretation upon a stated probability basis indicates a satisfactory population, by giving an objective measure of the work to be done, may permit municipalities which now require over-all bids to contract for the work on a per diem basis, or may at least permit contracts which specify a unit rate for the items in such tests, which would be the equivalent of a per diem rate for the accounts covered.

It is important to observe that considerations of cost are significant determinants of the specification of the hypotheses used in interpreting auditing samples and in selecting the probability levels on which the actual populations are to be accepted or rejected. This follows from the facts noted previously, namely, that raising the probability level on which decision is made increases the size of the minimum sample required and that the sample size is reduced as the gap between the two hypotheses used in sequential sampling is widened. The latter effort can be observed in table 12 (appendix ii). These remarks apply equally to the cost calculations of any particular audit and to the cost of auditing in general, which is discussed briefly in the succeeding section of this chapter. It is interesting to note that if the concepts of statistical sampling theory should become widely understood in the financial world it would be possible to render a certificate after the audit of a set of accounts in which the nature of the hypotheses used and the probability levels employed in interpreting the samples were disclosed, thus giving the reader a very precise indication of the quality of the audit in one of its fundamental aspects.

COST OF AUDITING IN GENERAL

It is obviously desirable that a balance be reached between the amount of auditing work (in terms of cost) and the consequences of not doing more. This can best be expressed in terms of a marginal computation: when, in general, the failure to extend auditing work a little bit further costs society (in terms of misdirected investments, fraud, etc.) slightly less than the additional auditing work would cost, the profession has arrived at the proper stopping point. The concept can be applied to any auditing situation, including a single engagement; in more general applications the idea can be, and in its essence is, applied to the whole practice of individual firms. As the last sentence indicates, the profession is already familiar with the need to reconcile the cost of auditing with its results. The purpose here is to indicate the theoretical possibility of calculating a sample size which achieves this balance; that is, a sample size which is most economical from the viewpoint of the cost of examining the items in it and the probabilities of failing to discover an unsatisfactory condition. Such a computation requires a formula which relates sample size and the costs of drawing samples with the costs incident to failure to discover objectionable conditions.

As an illustration, the following formula, which was devised for use in control of quality of manufactured product, is given:[5]

$$C = nT + P_m NM$$

where

C = cost of inspection plus average cost of misgrading
n = sample size
T = cost of selection and inspection of an article (entry, etc.)

---

[5] From Leslie R. Simon, *op. cit.*, pp. 108–109.

P_m = probability of misgrading a lot of articles (entries, etc.)
N = number of articles per lot
M = cost of misgrading an article (entry, etc.)

Use of the formula requires three things: establishment of an action limit, b, which results in rejection of samples where, for example, $\dfrac{C+1}{n+2} \geq b$, C being the number of defective articles in a sample; the calculation of unit costs which are more or less intangible in many manufacturing applications, but especially so in auditing; and the manipulation of the formula by the methods of differential calculus to find the value of n for which C is a minimum.

In view of the intangible character of the cost of failure to discover an unsatisfactory condition in auditing and the difficulties for the nonmathematician in evaluating such a formula, it is not believed that the accounting practitioner will be able to use this device, and it is mentioned here as a possible tool of research should the profession in its organized capacity desire to undertake studies of the general costs of auditing.

CHAPTER V

Drawing the Sample

RANDOMNESS

THE LAYMAN tends to think of a valid sample in terms of perfect representativeness; that is, of a sample which displays the pertinent characteristics of the population exactly—for example, one in which the percentage of errors is the same as in the population. Such a sample is indeed ideal, but it cannot be assumed to be in hand in any particular case in view of the obvious possibility of drawing a great variety of samples from one population. However, there are degrees of representativeness, and one writer on statistical subjects defines randomness as "... a sample that is representative of what we may expect to get if we take additional samples."[1] Many perfectly good samples are not representative in the sense that they display pertinent characteristics the same as or very close to those of the population, and, for practical application, we accordingly can define representativeness only in terms of probability.

The objective of any sampling process is to obtain data from which truthful conclusions about the population sampled may be made. The conclusions flow from the probability of drawing the particular sample. In order that inferences may be made upon the basis of probability calculations, it is necessary that samples be drawn so as to conform with the assumptions implicit in the mathematics used. Since we have defined probability as the ratio of certain events to all possible events in a series or set, it follows that we will be able to draw valid conclusions from samples only when all the possibilities are actually present, that is, *when each event in the set has an equal chance of being drawn for the sample each time an item is drawn.* The italicized clause is the definition of randomness

[1] W. A. Shewhart, *Economic Control of Quality of Manufactured Product* (New York, 1931), p. 410.

which will be used here. It follows, of course, that a random sample is one drawn under the conditions so specified. This definition of randomness may be linked to the quality of representativeness by pointing out that under these circumstances the sample drawn is more likely to reflect the characteristics of the population in the actual proportions they have in the population than in any other proportion.

Another approach to this point is the rule that bias should be avoided in drawing the sample. Bias is the existence of a selective factor; a child drawing from a bowl of red and black balls which he could see would usually draw more red balls, because he has a bias in favor of the bright color and for red in particular. The numerous devices invented by statisticians for the mechanical or objective drawing of samples are all designed to avoid bias. Personal bias, though prominent, is not the only form of bias by any means; in accounting records, for example, it is not uncommon to find a particular transaction recurring at regular intervals; thus we may find vouchers to reimburse petty cash made up weekly, or cash sales may be entered in the case receipts book daily. Under these circumstances a sample chosen, let us say, by taking every tenth entry may include a disproportionately large number of the recurring items if it happens to start at the right point, or, starting elsewhere, it may include none of them. In either case it is biased, not because of what it contains or does not contain, but because a selective factor was operating to determine the content in a particular way. In view of the need for randomness and the normal auditing practice of using samples drawn subjectively or on a spatial basis and the possibility that the bias present may be significant, it is well for auditors to give consideration to methods developed by statisticians for random drawing of samples.

Drawing with Replacement: Random Sampling Numbers

The most prominent device of general applicability for the drawing of a random sample where the items in the population can be given a numerical designation is a table of random sampling numbers.

Since the numbers in the table are arranged in random order, selection of a sample may be made by taking those items in the population that bear the numbers given by a section of the table. Random sampling numbers are available in three publications which are listed in the bibliography appended; the general form of the tables and the method of use appears in table 5 and the following remarks.

TABLE 5

RANDOM SAMPLING NUMBERS*

1	2	3	4
25621	94516	83513	97263
78134	37324	90265	75810
08964	29810	28106	39248
93705	67058	74497	10456
30573	23602	38517	25815
78126	73564	15080	36042
06481	71089	26974	19096
42599	51489	23964	73487
71322	54725	76321	21420
65458	63819	78059	45870
18697	97406	44892	63197
40930	30812	31065	68593

* This table was drawn by the author by means of a card-shuffling technique. Since it is intended for illustrative use only, it has not been tested for randomness.

Table 5 may be used to draw a sample of 10 from a population of 99 as an indication of the mode of operation. The first step is to recognize that the highest number of the population contains two digits, and to select a series of two-digit numbers in the table which will determine the sample. This may most conveniently be done by using the first two single columns in the table, and by beginning at the top and working down. The second step is to tabulate the numbers of the items in the sample by reading them from the table. Following this course we get a sample of 10 with these numbers: 25, 78, 8, 93, 30, 78, 6, 42, 71, 65.

It may be observed that none of the above items represents duplications in the sample; no number is drawn twice. However, if the same procedure had been used to draw a sample of 24, we would have taken the first 12 items from the first two columns and the second 12 from the third and fourth columns of the table, and we would have drawn the number 93 a second time. This discloses an important characteristic of random sampling tables: they give samples equivalent to those obtained by drawing single items from a population and replacing each item physically and mixing thoroughly before another item is drawn. The significance of this seemingly superstitious method is that it satisfies the mathematical assumption that each item in the population has an equal chance of being drawn at each stage, and, where the sample is interpreted by means of the binomial distribution, the method enables samples to be taken in a way which satisfies the assumption that the drawing is proceeding from a population with a certain percentage of errors. In a population which was small relative to the sample, the removal of a number of items for the sample might leave the population distinctly different from what it was at the start, so that remaining items could not be assumed to have been drawn from the same population as the first ones. The use of random sampling numbers therefore permits the binomial distribution to be used with rigorous accuracy, and where random numbers are used, the limitation upon the size of the sample relative to the population, which was placed at 10 per cent in previous references, may be ignored. Where an item appears a second or third time in a sample as a result of drawing with replacement, it is of course tabulated according to its quality (good or bad) two or three times; for example, if item 93 in the sample of 24 was an erroneous calculation and all the other items in the sample were correct, we would interpret the sample as one with 22 correct and 2 erroneous items.

Cases will occur in the experience of almost any user of a table of random sampling numbers in which the simple, straightforward procedure outlined above will "waste" many of the numbers, and simple devices may be used to avoid this. Suppose, for example, that the population from which it was desired to draw a sample of 10 totaled 125 items. The simple technique used above would cause the operator to use three columns of figures, and to reject the first

two numbers—256 and 781—as too large; to take the next one as
89, to reject the next three—937, 305, and 781—and so on. This
skipping may be avoided by deducting the largest multiple of the
population which can be taken from any number which the table
provides, and using the remainder as the determiner of the item to
be taken into the sample. In a population of 125, table 5 would give
a sample containing item 6 (from 256 minus 250 = 6), 31 (from
781), 89 (from 089), 62 (from 937), etc. Where the population
total is 100 or 1,000 or any other positive, integral power of 10, the
last item in the population (item 100 or 1,000, etc.) may be dropped
from consideration and the number of columns of numbers required
to be used in the table reduced by one, thus eliminating the possibility of finding larger numbers in the table than the population
affords. For example, in drawing samples from a population of 100
by this method the first item drawn, using the first two columns of
the table, would be item 25, and the sample would contain the same
items as though the population had 99, not 100, items. The samples
obtained by this method would be different from those obtained by
another, but the only error involved is the exclusion of one number
of the population, and that may be ignored.

Additional time-saving devices may be invented by the user, and
he may take an almost infinite variety of samples from a comparatively limited table of numbers by running through the table verti-
cally, then horizontally, then at various diagonals, etc., and by
starting at a variety of points. These possibilities give the tables a
validity for auditing which they could not otherwise possess, since
it means that the auditor's sample from any area of the accounts
cannot be anticipated by third parties by reference to the published
tables.

Various devices may be used to apply the tables to auditing situations. In those cases where the auditing consists of the examination
of a sample from a series of documents, as in vouching cash disbursements with checks or with voucher forms to which supporting
data are attached, or in the examination of sales invoices, a series of
numbers will usually be available on the documents. Here the body

of items from which the drawing is made will be defined by a series of numbers running from the first item entered during the period under review through the last one, and the number by which an item can be identified for purposes of using the table can either be taken as it appears in the client's records or as that number minus the last number used in the prior period. In the first case many numbers in the tables will be wasted because they are too small; in the second the operator gets a series of numbers for the population running from 1 to the total in the series being examined. Thus if a sample were drawn from a series of vouchers numbered 5608 through 6891, the auditor might use the first alternative and (referring to table 5) take as the first item voucher 6545, that being the first number in the series formed by the first four columns of the table falling within the numbers 5608 to 6891. Using the second alternative, he would calculate the numbers from which he was drawing as $6891 - 5608 = 1283$ numbers; the first one drawn would then be item number 896, or voucher number $5608 + 896 - 1 = 6503$. Obviously the use of differences of random numbers over a whole multiple of the number in the series under examination may be used here as before. The deduction of 1 in the foregoing computation may be avoided by using the last number of the prior period—in this case 5607—as the starting point in any calculation of a number.

Where the auditor's raw material is not given a numerical designation in the regular accounting routine, it may be given one by the auditor, and in many cases where a sampling technique is appropriate this will be relatively easy. In cash receipts entries, a daily deposit is common, and the auditor may draw a sample of deposit slips by use of the tables merely by designating the deposits with the number of the business day or even the number of the calendar day of the year in which they are made—a numerical sequence frequently published on calendars. Where inventory calculations are involved, numbers may be given to individual items by taking the average—or some standard—number of entries per sheet and multiplying by the number of sheets preceding the one in hand and then adding the number of lines to the item in question which precede it on the sheet. Since the sheets are usually numbered and the lines can be measured on a simple scale instead of counted, the process of numeration is easy.

In this connection it will be observed that some time is required to use the tables and to obtain the numbers of the series being examined, as well as to search the records for the items turned up in the sample defined by the table. This process is longer than the frequently employed method of examining a cluster of items—as, for example, all the canceled checks for the month of May. There is a circumstance which mitigates in favor of the use of tables, however, in addition to the need for a genuinely random sample. This is the possibility of "drawing" the sample in advance of the work in the client's office. Given the number of the last voucher used in the year preceding, the ones to be examined could be determined from the tables of random sampling numbers even before the vouchers were prepared; this work could be done during any slack time available by personnel of junior rank in the accounting office. Such a procedure has two additional advantages: it would give excellent assurance of compliance with the currently discussed standard for care in preparation of the auditing program, and it would avoid the bias so likely to be present in the personal selection of any individual auditor, which is especially important when, as often happens, the accountant in charge is not rotated on engagements.

STRATIFIED SAMPLING

It is possible to improve the representativeness of a sample by use of the method of stratified sampling.[2] This method is available wherever the population can be divided into mutually exclusive strata. In auditing applications the stratification can be made upon the basis of the size of the amounts in the transactions or calculations being examined. The procedure requires that proportions of the population falling into each category be known, and that samples taken from each category be related in size by the same proportions.

---

[2] Authority for this statement may be found in H. L. Rietz, ed., *Handbook of Mathematical Statistics* (Boston, 1924), p. 84.

Thus if 30 per cent of the extensions of an inventory are more than $5,000, a sample of 100 should be selected for the purposes of stratified sampling by drawing 30 items from the less than $5,000 group.

The results obtained in the samples from the several strata are combined for interpretation with respect to the whole population by taking a weighted average of them, the weights being the proportions of the population falling into the different strata, which pro-

TABLE 6

STRATIFIED SAMPLE

(1) Per cent of population represented	(2) Number of errors found	(1) × (2)
20	3	0.6
30	2	0.6
50	4	2.0
100	9	3.2

portions also determine the relative size of the samples taken from each stratum. Accordingly, a set of three samples taken from three strata representing 20 per cent, 30 per cent, and 50 per cent of a population, showing the number of errors indicated, would be combined as shown in table 6.

The result is interpreted as though 3.2 errors had been found in a sample of 100 taken randomly from the whole population.[a] Interpreting this sample with table 10 when $p_2 = 0.03$ we find that rejection is called for. If desired, the table may be computed for fractional values and a closer decision made where the averaging process provides fractional values for the errors. Where stratified sampling is to be used in connection with the sequential method the best procedure presumably will be to draw a minimum sample for sequential interpretation from the two or more strata, in the ratio determined by the strata, and, if further sampling is required, to

[a] Of course, only whole numbers of errors can be found but this does not interfere with the use of an average which is expressed as a fraction.

draw in groups of 10 or more from the several strata as before—
thus, if the proportions were 40 and 60, additional groups of 10
would be taken in the number of 4 from one strata and 6 from the
other. Drawing of several items at a time may always be practiced;
the possibility of interpretation at each step does not have to be
exercised.

The technique of stratified sampling offers to auditing an opportunity to combine the investigation of items in a population that are
considered especially significant—and that, therefore, are to be examined either completely or at least much more extensively than a
general sampling procedure requires—with the sampling of the population as a whole by means of the procedures advanced in this work.
Suppose, for example, that there are 250 individual invoices of
$1,500 or more charged to plant and equipment accounts in a par-
ticular case for the period under review, and that an additional 1,000
invoices of lesser amount have been entered for the same period. It
is desired to know whether the charges to capital accounts are justified, but examination of all invoices is uneconomical. Those of
$1,500 and more, however, are examined completely because of
the amounts involved. In this case it would be possible to extend the
examination somewhat and to be able to make a decision about the
probable extent of errors in the whole group of items. It does not
follow that a satisfactory condition in the larger items indicates a
similar situation among the smaller ones. Of course, the two groups
may be sampled separately. Where an over-all index is desired, the
computation, as before, requires a weighted average, but the number of errors found in the examination of the 250 large items cannot
be used directly unless it is zero, since samples proportional to the
population strata would require a complete examination of the
smaller items also. However, the minimum sample required under
the stipulations of table 10, where $p_2 = 0.03$, is 89. The use of stratified sampling in the present illustration would require that 18 items,
or 20 per cent, of the 89 be taken from the large items and 71, or
80 per cent, from the small ones. To obtain a sample of the entire
population which could be interpreted as a stratified sample, it

would therefore be necessary to draw 71 items from the group of smaller values. This would then be averaged with a sample of 18 with the number of errors determined by taking the same percentage of 18 as was found in the 250 actually examined. Thus, if 15 errors were found in the 250, 6 per cent, or 1.1, would be taken as the errors in the sample of 18 derived for purposes of the weighted average, and the final computations, assuming 2 errors to be found in the sample of 71, would be as follows:

$$20 \text{ per cent} \times 1.1 = 0.22$$
$$80 \text{ per cent} \times 2.0 = 1.60$$
$$\overline{1.82}$$

This number of errors in a sample of 89 indicates that the result is inconclusive and more samples must be taken to reach a decision.

The technique of stratified sampling gives a better estimate of the condition of the population than does unrestricted random sampling,[4] and, in cases where a substantial proportion of the population is examined completely because of the materiality of the items in the accounts, it furnishes a convenient basis for extending the work somewhat to obtain a more general result.

Customary Auditing Samples and Statistical Theory

It has been noted previously that auditors draw samples by subjective processes.[5] One result of this procedure is that auditing samples frequently are not taken on a random basis.[6] It is the purpose of this section to indicate some of the common departures from random sampling methods which are made by auditors, in order that the need for more attention to this factor may be apparent.

A tendency to examine material items and to make no examination of the smaller ones has been noted in the preceding section. This incomplete examination does not give an adequate basis for drawing conclusions for the whole population. There is no quarrel with the desire to examine the material items more thoroughly than the less

---

[4] Rietz, *op. cit.*

[5] See, for example, chapter iii, the section on accounts receivable.

[6] See A. W. Holmes, *Auditing Principles and Procedure*, pp. 102–103.

significant ones, but the latter must be included in at least a proportion of a minimum sample corresponding to their number in the
population if conclusions for the whole population are to be drawn.
This necessity is of obvious importance where there is some disposi-
tion to manipulate the accounts and the auditor's preoccupation with
the larger items is known, but it is also pertinent generally, since it
is reasonable to believe that more care will be taken with large items
than with small ones.

Specific practices in the examination of the major areas of the
accounts may be noted. It is a commonplace to find an inventory instruction which requires the selection of a certain number of items
per page or per book, or which specifies that every tenth item or
every item at some other interval be taken. The examination of
checks, cash disbursement vouchers, cash receipts, and sales records
almost invariably is conducted by taking all the transactions for a
period of time—one or two months are the commonest periods for
the first three items and a week is more commonly used for sales.
Practices differ between accounting firms and with the nature of the
client's operations, as well as otherwise, but the use of a time interval
as the basis for selection of the sample is all but universal for the
accounts named. Capital and maintenance expenditures are most
commonly investigated by restricting attention largely, if not wholly,
to the larger items.

The danger of being misled by a biased sample obtained as a result of the practices just named is evident, especially where a time
interval is taken for drawing the sample. The conditions under which
the accounts are kept may change during the course of a year and
the restriction of the sample to one set of the conditions may conceal
significant deficiencies in the others. Here again the most obvious
possibility lies in manipulation of the accounts, where restriction
of the sample to only one of the eleven months other than the closing
month suggests to the manipulator that if he only picks the right
month, a whole series of false entries may be overlooked. It is true,
as indicated previously, that statistical methods of the kind here
described do not permit an assurance that fraud will be discovered,

but their use, so far as the taking of a random sample is a requirement, will serve two useful purposes: the random sample will give the greatest opportunity to uncover the fraud, if it exists and so far as a balance sheet audit can uncover it; and the use of random samples will have the effect of deterring the manipulator somewhat in view of the fact that with them he cannot make any deductions on what items the sample will or will not contain. Such deductions can of course be made from knowledge of the period selected by the auditor in the prior year and from the common reluctance to take as the second month to be examined one which is adjacent to the closing month, which is examined largely as a means of confirming the adequacy of the closing process (the "cutoff"), rather than as a sample of the year's operations. The only conclusion which seems tenable to the author is that auditors' samples, as now taken, are so frequently biased as to make it difficult to defend the use of such sampling methods in auditing, and that the use of random samples would make the profession's defense of its methods much easier even if no other end was served.

SUBJECTIVE RANDOMIZING

The term "subjective randomizing" seems to be a contradiction in terms, since subjectivity has been described as introducing personal bias into the selection of samples, and the quality of randomness requires that no bias of any kind be present. It is possible, however, that samples may be drawn by an individual without exercising any significant bias in the operation, and the opportunities for doing this seem greater in auditing than in many other fields for which the statisticians have rejected any subjective method. In taking a sample of potatoes with the object of measuring their average weight, for example, the operator who proceeds visually to select the potatoes he will weigh may tend to pick potatoes which look to be of average weight, or to include a proportion of little ones and of big ones which seem to him to correspond with their proportions in the population. Such efforts proceed on his estimates, however, which may be wrong, and the result may be far from the truth desired. In auditing, however, the operator cannot "see" the attribute of the item he selects when drawing for a sample; he must examine the item by regular auditing procedures before it can be classified. He cannot therefore exercise any kind of choice as to items which do and do not represent errors, and since the tabulation of this attribute is the objective of the sampling, it may be exhibited satisfactorily in the sample even though some forms of personal bias were present in the drawing. In other words, the likelihood of significant bias on the part of the operator appearing in auditing samples chosen by an accountant conscious of the need for randomness in the sample seems to be rather slight.

This possibility may appeal to the profession as a practical substitute for the use of random sampling numbers or some similar device.[7] It should be used, if at all, only after the accountant is conscious of the significance of randomness and of course it excludes the use as a sample of all the items recorded in one time interval within the year, as well as the practice of drawing items at some fixed interval.

---

[7] Another device which might be used is a deck of cards with numbers, which could be shuffled and used as random sampling numbers are used. Mechanical devices for drawing numbers are another possibility.

APPENDICES

APPENDIX I

SUPPLEMENTAL INTRODUCTION TO THE NATURE OF
STATISTICAL INFERENCE

This appendix is provided for the reader who wishes a somewhat better understanding of the nature of the computation of probabilities and the reasoning proceeding from them than the main body of the text supplies. It is designed specifically to reënforce the ideas expressed in chapter i without attempting any general development of the subject.

TABLE 7

POSSIBLE RESULTS OF TOSSING ONE COIN TWICE

Possibilities on first toss	Consequent possibilities on second toss	Number of result
Heads............ {	Heads	1
	Tails	2
Tails............. {	Heads	3
	Tails	4

Computations of simple probability are familiar to most people, and perhaps the simplest example is the probability of obtaining heads on the toss of a single coin. This probability is one in two, or one half,[1] and illustrates the mathematical expression of probability—the ratio of certain events to all possible events in a series or set. The ratio can of course be expressed as a decimal (i.e., 0.5), and probabilities have usually been so stated throughout the present work.

It should be noted that the probability of getting a head on one toss of the coin and another head on a second toss is the product of their separate probabilities (i.e., $\frac{1}{2} \times \frac{1}{2} = \frac{1}{4}$, or 0.25), and that this can be arrived at by counting all the possible events from two successive tosses of the coin and taking the ratio of successful ones. The computation is shown in table 7.

It can be seen from the table that there can be four different results from the tossing of the coin: two heads, two tails, heads on the first toss with tails on the second, and tails on the first toss with heads on the second. Since only one of these results—the first—satisfies the condition defined as a "success" (two heads), and since four distinct events were possible, we arrive again at the probability of $\frac{1}{4}$ or 0.25.

The process of reasoning that is fundamental to the interpretation of

---

[1] Assuming that the coin is evenly weighted, that the tossing is not effectively manipulated, etc.

samples can be indicated from the foregoing data with the addition of a few details. Let us assume that there is a person who claims that, blindfolded, he can toss a coin twice and obtain two heads by use of a skill unique in him. The experiment is conducted with a coin furnished by someone not interested in protecting the performer; in other words, we have some reason to believe that the coin is genuine, or legal, and has the usual characteristics of coins, which we assume are evenly weighted, etc. The performer actually obtains two heads. Is this evidence that he has the special skill he claims? Statistical reasoning concludes that there is no evidence that he has such skill, *since the result obtained would be achieved 25 per cent of the time by chance alone.* On the other hand, if the performer obtained ten heads in succession, statistical reasoning would conclude that the result, though possible by chance, should not be attributed to chance since it would be obtained on a chance basis only about once in a thousand times (the probability is 0.000976+). In this case the observers would have to reëxamine their assumptions—that is, that the coin was genuine, that the performer could not see it, etc.—or conclude that he did have an extraordinary skill, such as the ability to determine which side was upward by feeling the coin and to toss it so that it would fall on the side he wanted.

A slightly more complicated case than the coin-tossing illustration, and one which is famous in statistical literature, is the psychic-medium case. Here a person claims to be able to identify the color of playing cards (red or black) as they are dealt, face down, from a deck. He offers to submit this power to a test in which a deck of six cards is to be used, the deck to contain three red and three black cards. As each card is dealt the medium indicates on which of two piles it is to be placed—that designated for red cards, or the one for black cards. He has no chance to see the faces of the cards. Here again the problem in judging any particular result is to determine the probability that it would occur by chance alone, and, therefore, to compute the number of ways in which the successful event could happen and the total number of possible events in the set. A tabulation of the ways in which the six cards in the present experiment could fall is given as table 8. One misplaced card gives rise to two errors—one in each pile. The letter R stands for a red card, B for a black one.

Any one of the tabulated arrangements may be the one drawn when the cards are dealt from a shuffled pack of three red and three black cards and placed as the medium directs. For purposes of the experiment the order in which the cards appear within the two piles is not significant, the important question being the number of misplaced cards as defined in the column headed "number of errors." The number of ways in which these errors can appear gives rise to the figures which express the probability of their appearance on a chance basis; in this case, the probability of no errors is 0.05, of two errors, 9/20 or 0.45, and the probability of getting either no errors or two errors is 0.5. Thus it may be concluded that a perfect performance

TABLE 8

POSSIBLE ARRANGEMENTS IN TWO PILES OF THREE RED AND THREE BLACK CARDS

Number of errors	Red position			Black position			Frequency of number of errors designated
	Order of drawing						
	1	2	3	4	5	6	
0.............	R	R	R	B	B	B	1
2............	R	R	B	R	B	B	9
	R	R	B	B	R	B	
	R	R	B	B	B	R	
	R	B	R	R	B	B	
	R	B	R	B	R	B	
	R	B	R	B	B	R	
	B	R	R	R	B	B	
	B	R	R	B	R	B	
	B	R	R	B	B	R	
4............	R	B	B	R	R	B	9
	R	B	B	R	B	R	
	R	B	B	B	R	R	
	B	R	B	R	R	B	
	B	R	B	R	B	R	
	B	R	B	B	R	R	
	B	B	R	R	R	B	
	B	B	R	R	B	R	
	B	B	R	B	R	R	
6.............	B	B	B	R	R	R	1
Total arrangements...							20

in such a test would not be evidence of special powers, since the result would happen by chance one time in twenty. The appropriateness of making a calculation such as the foregoing is emphasized when it is suggested that the medium might not claim infallibility, but might contend that one misplaced card was to be expected upon rare occasions, in which case his chance of success in one performance of this particular test is 50-50—a fact not obvious to casual observation! Here again repetition of the experiment or, alternatively, increasing the number of items in the sample—as by using twelve cards—would rapidly decrease the probability of a perfect or near-perfect performance by chance.

We are now ready to consider an illustrative case applicable, for some purposes, to actual auditing conditions. Consider a situation in which it is desired to interpret a sample of 25 taken from a set of 1,000 balls in a bowl, in which we have placed 100 white balls and 900 black balls. Obviously, we can draw 25 white balls, or 25 black balls, or any number of white balls from 1 to 24 with the rest black. If we conduct a large number of experiments by drawing 25 balls in order (replacing each one and mixing the lot after the one drawn is identified and tabulated), we will get results, on a chance basis alone, which are described mathematically as the binomial distribution.[2] A distribution merely tabulates items according to some classification, and in the present case the tabulation shows, as in the other illustrations, the probabilities of getting samples of 25 containing the number of white balls indicated. These have been computed directly from the formula for the binomial probability function, which is the mathematical expression of the ratio of successful to all possible events under the conditions stated: that is, two classes of objects (white and black balls) from which random drawings of a given number are made, with replacement after each item is drawn.[3] The distribution for the case in hand is given in table 9.

In this table three different probability computations are given: the first (column A) is the probability of drawing a single sample of 25 with the number of white balls indicated, and is the figure given by the formula; column B is obtained by accumulating the figures of column A for successive numbers of white balls, thus giving the probability that any sample of 25 will contain any number of white balls up to and including the number given on the line for which the probability figure is tabulated; column C gives complements of the figures of column B (one minus the column B probability figure), thus stating the probability of getting a sample with *more* white balls than the number indicated on the line of tabulation. Reference to the table indicates that we would expect to draw by chance in a sample of 25 a total of 4 or fewer white balls approximately 90 per cent of the time; correspondingly, we would expect to find more than 4 white balls in our sample of 25 approximately 10 per cent of the time. Since the probability of getting a sample with more than 11 white balls is less than 0.00001, or one chance in 100,000, these probabilities have not been tabulated.

It will be noted that we knew what we had in the bowl when we calculated

---

[2] The purpose of the replacement of each ball after it is drawn is to keep the ratio of white to black constant, and thus keep the character of the population unchanged.

[3] The formula is $Pr = {}_nC_r q^{n-r} p^r$, where Pr is the probability of getting a sample containing r white balls in drawing samples of n from a population in which the ratio of white balls is p and the ratio of black balls is q (of ocurse, $q = 1 - p$), and ${}_nC_r$ means the number of combinations which can be made of n things taken r at a time. The formula is derived from probability theory and may be found described in general works on statistical theory.

table 9. Obviously, neither the calculation nor the sampling process would be required if we had this knowledge in any practical case—it is, in fact, the knowledge we would prefer to secure from the sample. It is also evident that we cannot be absolutely sure of the precise character of the population without examining each item in it. These statements, however, do not defeat the

TABLE 9

PROBABILITIES OF DRAWING WHITE BALLS IN RANDOM SAMPLES OF 25 FROM A
POPULATION OF 100 WHITE AND 900 BLACK BALLS*

(sampling with replacement)

Number of white balls in the sample	Probability of drawing a sample with		
	A	B	C
	Indicated number of white balls	Indicated number of white balls or *fewer*	*More* than the indicated number of white balls
0..............................	0.07179	0.07179	0.92821
1..............................	0.19942	0.27121	0.72879
2..............................	0.26589	0.53710	0.46290
3..............................	0.22650	0.76360	0.23640
4..............................	0.13842	0.90202	0.09798
5..............................	0.06459	0.96661	0.03339
6..............................	0.02392	0.99053	0.00947
7..............................	0.00721	0.99774	0.00226
8..............................	0.00180	0.99954	0.00046
9..............................	0.00038	0.99992	0.00008
10.............................	0.00007	0.99999	0.00001
11.............................	0.00001	1.00000	0.00000
Total probability.............	1.00000	1.00000	1.00000

* Samples with more than 11 white balls are so rare as to appear less than 0.001 per cent of the time, and so are not tabulated. Although samples with more than 11 white balls can and will (very infrequently) appear, column A is nevertheless added to 1.0 (thus accounting, formally, for all probabilities) because the figures have been rounded to five decimal places and there are no figures in the fifth decimal place for any probability beyond 11 white balls in a sample.

usefulness of statistical interpretation of samples, but are given to clarify the method. The process of reasoning is as follows: we know something about the population we are planning to sample (in auditing we can classify our findings or samples into two classes—right and wrong entries or calculations—and so we know at least that our samples will represent a binomial distribution and we also know something of how the accounting is conducted), and upon this basis we can set up a hypothesis (make an assumption about the population) *which we will test with our sample.* If the sample gives us no reason to doubt the propriety of our hypothesis, we may let the hypothesis stand as our decision about the character of the population.[4] For example, if we had not known the ratio of white to black balls in the bowl (one to nine), we could have set up the hypothesis that 10 per cent of the balls were white. Suppose also that we desire to interpret the sample on a 99 per cent probability level, that is, we will calculate the results we expect to get 99 per cent of the time in sampling the hypothetical population, and compare the sample with this figure. Table 9 gives the distribution of samples of 25 from the postulated population; in the second probability column we look for 99 per cent. We find a near approximation to it on the line for 6 white balls. In other words, we expect to find 6 white balls *or fewer* 99 per cent of the time. If, then, we actually draw 8, we would be inclined to reject the hypothesis that the population actually had only 10 per cent white balls.

Use of a single probability form of the binomial distribution is satisfactory enough when we draw more than the highest number of white balls which we would expect to get 99 per cent of the time and so conclude that we cannot accept the hypothesis that the bowl had not more than 10 per cent white balls, since the sample would either have to be a very rare one from a 10 per cent population or a not-so-rare one from a population with more than 10 per cent white balls. Suppose, however, that we had drawn 5 white balls. We might then say that since the sample was within the limits we set up for our expectations we could accept the hypothesis that the population had not more than 10 per cent white balls. The objection to this conclusion is that many populations of distinctly more than 10 per cent white balls— say 12 per cent or 14 per cent—would give the same result—a sample of 25 with 5 white balls—relatively frequently. If we *accept* the hypothesis on such evidence, we have little ground for defending our choice of a hypothesis—an adjacent one would also have been accepted. We therefore need a more discriminating basis for accepting the postulated figure, and we found it in the likelihood ratio as applied by the formulas for sequential sampling which are presented for the binomial case in appendix ii.

Further information on the computation of probabilities and subsequent interpretation may be found in general texts on statistics, some of which are listed in the bibliography at the end of this volume.

---

[4] The adequacy of this procedure has been appraised and supplemented in the preceding sections.

APPENDIX II

THE LIKELIHOOD RATIO

Since the likelihood ratio is the basis for the sequential sampling method, a more formal description of it is given as an introduction to the formulas provided by sequential sampling; this will be useful also in defining the symbols used in the formulas and in the tables.

The likelihood ratio requires the use of two hypotheses, H_1, that the population has p_1 (percentage) defectives or fewer, and H_2, that it has p_2 (percentage) defectives or more. If the probability of drawing the sample from H_1 is P_1 and of drawing it from H_2 is P_2 the likelihood ratio is $\frac{P_2}{P_1}$. It should, be noted that we are not restricted to the same level of probability for accepting one hypothesis which we use in accepting the other. The level of risk we accept in making a decision (and we must accept some, or we will have to examine every item in the population) is therefore expressed in two parts. Following the literature we will designate the risk of accepting H_2 when H_1 is true as a (alpha) and the risk of accepting H_1 when H_2 is true as β (beta).

The estimates (H_1 and H_2) are set not with the intent of specifying exactly the character of the population (again, that is an impractical objective in most cases) but as action limits. That is, H_1 is set at a value which we are readily willing to consider satisfactory in the population, whereas H_2 is set at a value which represents a definitely unacceptable population. This resolves the difficulty of making a decision upon the basis of simple probability alone. Whereas in simple probability an actual population just beyond, say, 3 per cent of allowable errors might frequently give a sample which could frequently come from a population of 3 per cent defective or slightly less and so lead us to a wrong conclusion of acceptance, such a condition no longer results—at least so readily—in acceptance; the computation on the 3 per cent hypothetical population now serves primarily as a basis for *rejection,* and *acceptance* depends primarily on a considerably more nearly perfect population—the H_1 of our earlier expression. Thus if we set H_1 at 0.01 per cent (almost no errors) and H_2 at 3 per cent and take a 10 per cent risk of wrong decisions, we will find that we cannot accept a sample of 100 showing 4 errors as likely to come from a population of 0.01 per cent or fewer errors, whereas we could accept the population as one having 3 per cent *or fewer* errors if we made the interpretation on simple probability alone, because we expect to draw up to and including 4 errors in 90 per cent of our drawings from a binomial population not more than 3 per cent defective. In this connection, it should be observed that, following the method of sequential sampling outlined below, actual populations of very few errors will be quickly accepted;

those with high proportions of errors will be quickly identified as beyond the rejection point; and those which fall in between the H_1 and H_2 selected will require the largest amount of examination (the largest sample to be taken) before a decision can be reached. This is as it should be; in auditing terms accounts which can be readily certified or seen to be inadequate for any certification will be readily isolated, whereas those which may be certified after careful examination (to identify and eliminate the substantial but nevertheless manageable errors) will require extensive examination before the certificate can be given.

SEQUENTIAL SAMPLING

In terms of procedure, sequential sampling is a process using the likelihood ratio in which one of three conclusions can be reached after any single item is drawn and inspected for the sample. These conclusions are (1) that the population is acceptable, (2) that it is not acceptable, or (3) that the evidence up to that point is inconclusive. Mathematically, the method takes each observation into account, incorporating each one as it is drawn into the computation of the likelihood ratio so that one of the three possible conclusions is indicated at each stage of the drawing.

The method may be used in a graphical procedure: two lines are drawn on the chart to define the areas in which the three possible conclusions from the sampling are to be found. The lines are parallel and the chart has the following general appearance:

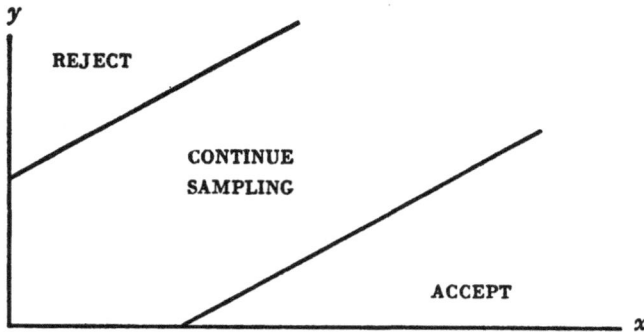

As sampling proceeds under this device, a dot is placed on the chart corresponding, on the x axis, to the number of items drawn up to that point, and on the y axis, to the number of errors observed up to that point. When the dot falls on or below the lower parallel line, the population is accepted as being more likely of the character of H_1 (0.01 per cent defectives or fewer in the illustration given above); if it falls on or above the upper line the population is taken to be unacceptable (as more likely to be of the character of H_2); and if it falls within the two lines the likelihood ratio is not conclusive and sampling must continue if a decision to accept or reject is to be reached.

The formulas by which the graph is constructed for the binomial case (when the population is classifiable in two categories—as right and wrong entries) are as follows:

The two lines are defined as

$$y_1 = -h_1 + sx \text{ (lower line)}$$
$$y_2 = h_2 + sx \text{ (upper line)}$$

where

$x =$ number of items in the sample,
$s =$ the common slope and
$-h_1$ and h_2 are the y intercepts.

The intercepts and slope are defined as follows:

$$h_1 = \frac{\log\left(\frac{1-a}{\beta}\right)}{\log\frac{p_2}{p_1}\left(\frac{1-p_1}{1-p_2}\right)}$$

$$h_2 = \frac{\log\left(\frac{1-\beta}{a}\right)}{\log\frac{p_2}{p_1}\left(\frac{1-p_1}{1-p_2}\right)}$$

$$s = \frac{\log\left(\frac{1-p_1}{1-p_2}\right)}{\log\frac{p_2}{p_1}\left(\frac{1-p_1}{1-p_2}\right)}$$

Formulas which simplify the calculation of these values are as follows:

$$g_1 = \log\frac{p_2}{p_1} \qquad\qquad A = \log\frac{1-\beta}{a}$$

$$g_2 = \log\frac{1-p_1}{1-p_2} \qquad\qquad B = \log\frac{1-a}{\beta}$$

Then

$$h_1 = \frac{B}{g_1 + g_2} \qquad\qquad s = \frac{g_2}{g_1 + g_2}$$

$$h_2 = \frac{A}{g_1 + g_2}$$

These symbols have the same meanings given earlier:

p_1 = proportion of defectives in the desirable hypothesis (H_1)
p_2 = proportion of defectives in the alternative hypothesis (H_2)
a = the risk of accepting H_2 when H_1 is true
β = the risk of accepting H_1 when H_2 is true

The logarithms used are the common logs to the base 10. Although the graphical procedure is of some use in sampling practice and for purposes of exposition, accountants may prefer to use tables. These tables may be constructed for whatever values of a, β, H_1, and H_2 are desired, the simplest procedure being to solve the equations of the two lines for appropriate values of x and y. Tables which further simplify the calculations involved are to be had in S. R. G. Report 255. Table 2.21 of the report (p. 2.37) gives A and B in terms of a and β. The characteristics of sequential sampling may be observed in table 2.23 (p. 2.39 ff.), which gives the intercepts, slope, minimum sample sizes for acceptance and rejection, and average sample sizes where H_1 is true and where H_2 is true for a number of values of the variables. The first of these tables is reproduced in the present work as table 11, page 92; and excerpts from the second are reproduced as table 12, p. 93. The latter table gives values for h_1, h_2, and s for related values of p_1 and p_2 where $a = 0.05$ and $\beta = 0.10$, and so may be used to write formulas for the lines which determine the action points appropriate to any sample size.

Table 10 is drawn to illustrate the tabular procedure for using sequential sampling and to serve practical auditing use so far as auditors may be willing to accept the hypotheses represented in it. The table was obtained from the formulas given above, the lines for $p_1 = 0.005$ and $p_2 = 0.03$ being

$$y_1 = -1.238880 + 0.014018\,x$$
$$y_2 = 1.590564 - 0.014018\,x$$

and the lines for $p_1 = 0.005$ and $p_2 = 0.05$ being

$$y_1 = -0.958447 + 0.019716\,x$$
$$y_2 = 1.230524 + 0.019716\,x$$

with $a = 0.05$ and $\beta = 0.10$ in each case.

The first column in each section lists the number in the sample to any point; the second column gives the number of defects in it which indicate acceptance, and the third column gives the number of defects which indicate rejection. When the number of defects accumulated reaches either point for the corresponding sample the indicated conclusion is taken, but so long as the number of defects falls between the two figures the sampling is continued. The figures for the defects are computed from the formulas for the lines stated immediately above by taking as the number of defects for acceptance at any sample number the value of y_1 (fractions are raised to the next integer) at that point (x = number in sample), and the number for acceptance is the corresponding point on y_2 (fractions are reduced to the nearest integer). Reference to the chart will clarify this. In using the chart it may be borne in mind that although "acceptance" or "rejection" is at some point indicated, the auditor may nevertheless continue the sampling if he has any reason to be dissatisfied with the result; if the original result was due to drawing a rare sample, increasing the size of the sample will tend to make it more representative and may change the conclusion.

TABLE 10

ACTION POINTS FOR SEQUENTIAL TESTS*

(When $a = 0.05$, $\beta = 0.10$ and p_1 and p_2 Have the Values Shown)

$p_1 = 0.005$, $p_2 = 0.03$			$p_1 = 0.005$, $p_2 = 0.05$		
n	y_1 (accept)	y_2 (reject)	n	y_1 (accept)	y_2 (reject)
2	..	2	2	..	2
29	..	2	39	..	2
89	0	3	49	0	3
100	0	3	89	0	3
160	1	4	100	1	4
171	1	4	140	1	4
239	2	5	151	2	5
243	2	5	191	2	5
303	3	6	201	3	6
314	3	6	241	3	6
374	4	7	252	4	7
385	4	7	292	4	7
446	5	8	303	5	8
457	5	8	343	5	8
517	6	9	353	6	9
528	6	9	384	6	9
588	7	10	404	7	10
599	7	10	440	7	10

$$y_1 = -1.238880 + 0.014018\,x$$
$$y_2 = 1.590564 + 0.014018\,x$$

$$y_1 = -0.958447 + 0.019716\,x$$
$$y_2 = 1.230524 + 0.019716\,x$$

* Explanation of symbols: a is the maximum risk of rejecting a population of p_1 when it is the fact; β is the maximum risk of accepting a population of p_1 when p_2 is the fact; $p_1 =$ the proportion of defectives allowable in a definitely acceptable population; $p_2 =$ the proportion of defectives which cannot be tolerated in the population; $n =$ the number in the sample; $y_1 =$ the maximum number of defects which may appear in the sample with acceptance of the population as most likely p_1; $y_2 =$ the number of defects in the sample which are necessary to indicate the population as most likely p_2.

Notes on use of the table: Where leaders appear in the y_1 or y_2 columns, no decision can be made (to accept, in the above table, since the sample is too small).

For sample sizes which fall between any two sizes noted above (column n), take the preceding number given in column y_1, and in column y_2 take the following entry. Example: for samples of 250 (left-hand table) accept if 2 or less errors are found, reject if 6 errors or more are found.

TABLE 11

A AND B IN TERMS OF α AND β*

$$A = \log\frac{1-\beta}{\alpha}$$

$$B = \log\frac{1-\alpha}{\beta}$$

		α for computing A, β for computing B									
		0.001	0.01	0.02	0.03	0.04	0.05	0.10	0.15	0.20	0.30	0.40
β for computing A, α for computing B	0.001.........	3.000	2.000	1.699	1.522	1.398	1.301	1.000	0.823	0.699	0.522	0.398
	0.01.........	2.996	1.996	1.695	1.519	1.394	1.279	0.996	0.820	0.695	0.519	0.394
	0.02.........	2.991	1.991	1.690	1.514	1.389	1.292	0.991	0.815	0.690	0.514	0.389
	0.03.........	2.987	1.987	1.686	1.510	1.385	1.288	0.987	0.811	0.686	0.510	0.385
	0.04.........	2.982	1.982	1.681	1.505	1.380	1.283	0.982	0.806	0.681	0.505	0.380
	0.05.........	2.978	1.978	1.677	1.501	1.376	1.279	0.978	0.802	0.677	0.501	0.376
	0.10.........	2.954	1.954	1.653	1.477	1.352	1.255	0.954	0.778	0.653	0.477	0.352
	0.15.........	2.929	1.929	1.628	1.452	1.327	1.230	0.929	0.753	0.628	0.452	0.327
	0.20.........	2.903	1.903	1.602	1.426	1.301	1.204	0.903	0.727	0.602	0.426	0.301
	0.30.........	2.845	1.845	1.544	1.368	1.243	1.146	0.845	0.669	0.544	0.368	0.243
	0.40.........	2.778	1.778	1.477	1.301	1.176	1.079	0.778	0.602	0.477	0.301	0.176

*Example of use of table: If α = 0.04, β = 0.01, find column headed 0.04 and row 0.01. The common element gives A = 1.394. Find row headed 0.04 and column 0.01. The common element gives B = 1.982.

In general, in finding A, α is the column heading and β is the row heading; in finding B, α is the row heading and β the column heading.

TABLE 12

CHARACTERISTIC QUANTITIES OF SEQUENTIAL TESTS FOR THE BINOMIAL
DISTRIBUTION COMPUTED FOR VARIOUS COMBINATIONS OF p_1 AND p_2*

(Where $a = 0.05$ and $\beta = 0.10$)

p_1	p_2	h_2	h_1	s	m_0	m_1	$\bar{n}p_1$	$\bar{n}p_2$
0.001	0.02	0.958681	0.746711	0.006373	118	1	123	58
0.001	0.03	0.842512	0.656227	0.008588	77	1	77	32
0.001	0.04	0.775169	0.603774	0.010673	57	1	57	22
0.001	0.05	0.729465	0.568176	0.012698	45	1	45	16
0.001	0.06	0.695600	0.541799	0.014658	37	1	37	13
0.0025	0.02	1.378240	1.073503	0.008460	127	2	160	98
0.0025	0.03	1.150239	0.895913	0.011144	81	2	92	50
0.0025	0.04	1.028270	0.800913	0.013645	59	2	64	32
0.0025	0.05	0.949368	0.739457	0.016026	47	1	48	23
0.0025	0.06	0.892801	0.695397	0.018348	38	1	39	18
0.005	0.02	2.062373	1.606370	0.010834	149	3	244	185
0.005	0.03	1.590564	1.238880	0.014018	89	2	122	82
0.005	0.04	1.366441	1.064313	0.016948	63	2	79	49
0.005	0.05	1.230524	0.958447	0.019716	49	2	58	33
0.005	0.06	1.137154	0.885722	0.022368	40	2	45	25
0.0075	0.02	2.909251	2.265997	0.012802	177	3	379	330
0.0075	0.03	2.051030	1.597535	0.016275	99	3	161	123
0.0075	0.04	1.692977	1.318649	0.019527	68	2	97	68
0.0075	0.05	1.489204	1.159932	0.022531	52	2	68	45
0.0075	0.06	1.354573	1.055069	0.025492	42	2	52	32
0.01	0.02	4.109755	3.201062	0.014430	222	5	640	607
0.01	0.03	2.582914	2.011815	0.018222	111	3	217	181
0.01	0.04	2.039688	1.588700	0.021749	73	5	120	92
0.01	0.05	1.751023	1.363861	0.024982	55	2	81	58
0.01	0.06	1.567807	1.221155	0.028116	44	2	60	40
0.02	0.03	6.952267	5.415076	0.024648	220	8	1032	1071
0.02	0.05	3.050966	2.376378	0.032840	73	4	164	146
0.02	0.10	1.705649	1.328520	0.050259	27	2	39	28
0.03	0.04	9.698312	7.553953	0.034715	218	11	1420	1524
0.03	0.05	5.436236	4.234249	0.039272	108	6	405	413
0.03	0.10	2.260088	1.760368	0.058584	31	3	55	45

*Note. m_0 = smallest sample number for which acceptance is possible.
m_1 = smallest sample number for which rejection is possible.
$\bar{n}p_1$ = average sample size if the population is of the quality of p_1.
$\bar{n}p_2$ = average sample size if the population is of the quality of p_2.
Other symbols have the meanings given in the text.

APPENDIX III

The first promulgation of auditing standards resulted from the desire for a uniform system of accounting on the part of government procurement officers during World War I, and particularly of members of the Federal Trade Commission. The project was discussed with members of the American Institute of Accountants, who considered a uniform system of accounts an impractical objective, but took the suggestion as an opportunity to inform businessmen of the desirability of audits and to improve the practice of statement presentation. A booklet was prepared which stated the fundamental procedures of auditing and presented well-accepted forms for the balance sheet and profit and loss statement. It was issued as a tentative proposal in the *Federal Reserve Bulletin* in 1917 under the title "Uniform Accounting" and subsequently reprinted under the title *Approved Methods for the Preparation of Balance Sheet Statements*. In this form it became famous as a statement of desirable auditing procedures and of statement forms. The nature of the material included can be judged by the reader not already familiar with the pamphlet from the quotation of the first sentence appearing under the caption "Cash": "The cash on hand preferably should be counted after banking hours on the last day of the fiscal period to be covered by the audit, and the amount thereof, together with the cash stated to be in bank, reconciled with that shown by the cashbook." It can be seen that the instructions follow generally the form of a brief textbook on auditing, and can serve as specific measures or standards of the work done in the pertinent parts of any audit.

The pamphlet was revised and reissued again by the Federal Reserve Board in 1929, this time under the title *Verification of Financial Statements*. Unmistakable indication of the fact that this and its preceding editions were intended to serve as standards—indeed, they could have no other purpose— is found in the preface of the 1929 issue, in which it is stated that "Accountants have a professional as well as a practical interest in a standard of procedure. Statements which are misleading or actually false tend to discredit accounting as a profession." Revisions were not extensive, perhaps the major one being a complete rewording of the certificate form suggested. The evolution of the certificate, or short-form report or opinion, can thus be traced from the genesis of all formally promulgated auditing standards in the United States.

Developments in the field of auditing were rapid after 1929. The financial debacle focused attention upon financial statements and the audits which gave assurance of their validity. The New York Stock Exchange began to require certified statements from listed corporations, and the wave of reform legislation brought the Securities and Exchange Commission upon the scene with requirements for more disclosure in financial reports. Shortly after the creation of the S. E. C. the profession revised the material formerly published by the Federal Reserve Board once more, and, in 1936, brought out under the imprint of the American Institute of Accountants the booklet entitled *Examination of Financial Statements by Independent Public Accountants.* Here the material was considerably expanded. In this publication the now familiar emphasis upon disclosure of accounting principles followed in the statements was introduced, and the equally familiar emphasis upon consistency in the use of accounting principles to obtain the statements was begun. A third point of departure appeared in the added attention given to the income account, although the original Federal Reserve publication had defined the scope of a balance sheet audit as including "a general examination of the profit and loss account." The 1936 booklet divided the discussion of the specific procedures between those appropriate to a small- or moderate-sized company, and the modifications of program required for use in the audit of a large company. Desirable statement forms were again included, and the form of certificate or "accountant's report" was expanded, in line with the need to make clear to readers the limitations of audits. The major part of the publication is the program of examination which suggests specific procedures without contending that they are the only acceptable ones. There is no doubt, however, that an accountant who ignores procedures suggested as desirable in the booklet should be placed on the defensive in justifying his neglect of them. This booklet is the only standard of comparable generality which gives specific procedures, but it is out of print and the publisher (The American Institute of Accountants) has moved away from sponsorship of specific procedures and, considering the booklet obsolete, evidently does not propose to reissue it.

The last in the pamphlet series of important statements on auditing procedure is a booklet published by the American Institute of Accountants in 1947. It is entitled *Tentative Statement of Auditing Standards* and is a special report of the Institute's Committee on Auditing Procedure. This statement avoids specifying any detailed auditing procedures as standards and confines the discussion to general objectives and qualifications of the auditor. The outline of this material follows:

General standards:
    1. Technical training and proficiency of the auditor.
    2. Independence in his mental attitude and approach.
    3. Due care in his performance.
Standards of field work:
    1. Adequacy of preparatory planning of field work.
    2. Proper evaluation of the existing internal control for reliance thereon and for the determination of the resultant extent of the tests to which auditing procedures are restricted.

3. Competence of evidential matter.

Standards of reporting:

1. Adherence to accepted principles and practices of accounting.
2. Observance of consistency in their application, except where conditions warrant otherwise.
3. Adequacy of informative disclosures in the financial statements, their scope and limitation.

This outline requires the addition of considerable detail before it can be applied to an individual case as a measure of performance.

A leading part in the movement to establish generally accepted auditing standards has been taken by two committees of the American Institute of Accountants, namely, the Committee on Auditing Procedure and the Committee on Accounting Procedure. The former committee initiated the extensions of auditing procedure adopted as generally accepted practice by the membership of the Institute in 1939, requiring physical contact with inventory and confirmation of accounts receivable by correspondence (both on a test basis). Each committee has issued more than twenty statements to date, and these bulletins constitute standards with which every public accountant should be familiar.

Several individual writers are prominent in the movement, but for present purposes only one need be noted. A leading role in developing accepted auditing standards has been taken by Samuel J. Broad, formerly Chairman of the Committee on Auditing Procedure of the American Institute of Accountants. In 1942 Mr. Broad proposed a statement of auditing standards that included brief requirements for the audit of the major balance sheet accounts and a paragraph stating that test checks of the operating accounts should be made to the degree necessary to satisfy the auditor, as well as some general statements with reference to accepted principles of accounting, consistency of application of accounting principles, and reliance upon internal control.[1] Recognition is given in the presentation of this material to the opinion of many accountants that standards should not be expressed in much detail for fear of unduly restricting professional judgment, and the statement is made with respect to the suggested standards, "Perhaps some of those I have listed are procedures rather than standards and should be excluded."[2] The question of the degree to which the whole body of auditing standards should be specific is not germane to the present work, but the writer ventures the opinion that a standard couched in general terms will merely state an objective rather than create a measure which can be effectively used by the courts, the regulative bodies, and the profession itself to judge individual auditing performances without tedious testimony in each case as to what application of the standard in the case should be.

[1] Samuel J. Broad, "Auditing Standards," *Journal of Accountancy*, LXXII (Nov., 1941), 390–397.

[2] *Ibid.*, p. 395.

Contrary opinions will be found in the publications listed in the bibliography appended to the present work. The literature is as yet small; six writers advocating formulation of standards, one opposed, and one documenting the subject rather than arguing it have been found by the author in the leading journals. The opposing attitude is perhaps best expressed in a quotation from the *Accountant* (London) of August 16, 1941: "... auditing is a job which, by its very nature, must rely less on general statements of principle than on adaptations of variable technique to meet the almost incredible heterogeneity of factual combinations making up the material on which auditors must work. That is why, in England, emphasis has always been laid more strongly on the personal equation in auditing than on an appeal to any code of operations laid down *in vacuo* by external authority." The English writer of course did not have the statistical theory of sampling in mind.

A major factor in the development of auditing standards in the United States is the Securities and Exchange Commission. Charged with the duty of seeing that adequate financial statements are available to buyers of most corporate securities traded in interstate commerce, the S. E. C. is logically interested in the adequacy of audits which testify to the fairness of statements, having, in fact, required all registration statements to be certified. In addition to exercising an indirect but potent influence upon auditing practice—as a result of regulations that require more disclosure in the published statements than have been generally available—the S. E. C. has established two groups of rules which directly regulate certain areas of auditing practice for reports filed with the Commission. The first of these is Article 2 of Regulation S-X, which deals with the qualifications of accountants and the form and content of their certificates. It is the requirement of independence expressed in this article which has given rise to the widespread discussion of this subject in recent years. The part of the article dealing with the form and content of the certificate includes the requirement that it be stated "whether the audit was made in accordance with generally accepted auditing standards applicable in the circumstances." This requirement has greatly stimulated the efforts of the profession to develop a statement of auditing standards which can be generally accepted. At the present time, however, such a statement is still under discussion, and standards must be identified in the somewhat uncorrelated materials available in the booklet entitled *Examination of Financial Statements,* in the bulletins of committees of the American Institute of Accountants, in the recommendations in textbooks, and in the opinions of individuals.

The second group of S. E. C. rules set up specific auditing standards in its "General Instructions with Respect to Form X-17A-5"; they consist of "Minimum Audit Requirements" for the financial statement filed by certain securities brokers and dealers. These procedures are specific, including, for example, the requirement that physical examination and comparison with books be made of all securities on hand, in vault, in box, or otherwise in physical possession of the broker. This particular group of requirements, being restricted to a small segment of auditing practice, has not been the subject of much discussion in the literature of the profession, but it constitutes a very definite standard in its field.

It is apparent, then, that the present status of auditing standards is in process of growth. There is an out-of-print booklet expressing minimum procedures which is the outgrowth of a long period of professional discussion stimulated by official interest, but the standard certificate or short form report suggested by the American Institute of Accountants provides the assertion that generally accepted auditing standards have been used without making any reference to this booklet, which indeed is considered obsolete. Additions have been made to the materials unmistakably constituting auditing standards by committees of the Institute but differences of opinion apparently prevent an integration in effective form. At the same time, the S. E. C. specifies certain standards it thinks necessary to be defined for practice before the Commission. It is easy to understand the fear of those who wish to avoid a detailed specification of their work, and it is to be hoped that means will be found—possibly through specification of alternative procedures and qualifications for special circumstances—for a standard to be formulated which will be powerful enough to support even the state boards in efforts toward improvement of the profession.

BIBLIOGRAPHY

BIBLIOGRAPHY

STATISTICAL METHODS IN GENERAL

CLOPPER, C. J., and E. S. PEARSON, "The Use of Confidence or Fiducial Limits Illustrated in the Case of the Binomial," *Biometrika*, XXVI (Dec., 1934).

CROXTON, FREDERICK E., and DUDLEY J. COWDEN, *Applied General Statistics*, New York, Prentice-Hall, Inc., 1945. 822 pp.

SHEWHART, WALTER A., *Economic Control of Quality of Manufactured Product*, New York, D. Van Nostrand Co., 1931. 501 pp.

SIMON, LESLIE E., *An Engineer's Manual of Statistical Methods*, New York, John Wiley & Sons, 1941. 219 pp.

SMITH, JAMES G., and ACHESON J. DUNCAN, *Sampling Statistics and Applications*, New York, McGraw-Hill Book Co., 1945. 455 pp.

Statistical Research Group, Columbia University, *Sequential Analysis of Statistical Data*, New York, Columbia University Press, 1945. Enlarged and published as *Sampling Inspection*, New York, McGraw-Hill Book Co., 1948. 395 pp. Originally printed as Report 255 of the Statistical Research Group, Columbia University, to the Applied Mathematics Panel, National Defense Research Committee, U. S. Office of Scientific Research and Development, 1944.

WILKS, S. S., "Confidence Limits and Critical Differences between Percentages," *Public Opinion Quarterly*, IV (June, 1940).

YULE, G. U., and M. G. KENDALL, *An Introduction to the Theory of Statistics*, 12th ed., rev., London, Charles Griffen & Co., 1940. 493 pp.

MATHEMATICAL OR STATISTICAL BASES FOR AUDITING SAMPLES

Note: The article by Lewis A. Carman listed below is the only one found by the present writer when the present work was begun presenting any original effort to make mathematical probability theory available to auditing use. It arrives at sample sizes as percentages of finite populations designed to enable the auditor to observe at least one fraudulent entry on varying probability levels upon the hypothesis that some absolute number of fraudulent entries from 1 to 40 existed in the population. It does not attempt a more general interpretation of the sample. The articles by Prytherch and Herbert listed below rely entirely upon Carman's for their presentation of material based upon mathematical probability. The articles by Abrams and Cranstown give relatively brief treatment of application of mathematical probability to auditing.

ABRAMS, JEROME, "Sampling Theory Applied to the Test-Audit," *New York Certified Public Accountant*, XVII (Oct., 1947), 645–652.

CARMAN, LEWIS A., "The Efficacy of Tests," *The American Accountant*, XVIII (Dec., 1933), 360–366.

CRANSTOWN, WILLIAM D., "A New Look at Basic Auditing Techniques," *The Journal of Accountancy*, LXXXVI (Oct., 1948), 274–283.

HERBERT, LEO, "Practical Sampling for Auditors," *The New York Certified Public Accountant*, XVII (Jan., 1947), 57–61.

NETER, JOHN, "An Investigation of the Usefulness of Statistical Sampling Methods in Auditing," *The Journal of Accountancy*, LXXXVII (May, 1949), 390–398.

PRYTHERCH, ROBERT H., "How Much Test Checking Is Enough?", *The Journal of Accountancy*, LXXIV (Dec., 1942), 525–530.

VANCE, LAWRENCE L., "Statistical Sampling Theory and Auditing Procedure: Problems and Applications," *Proceedings of the Pacific Coast Economic Association* (1947).

———, "Auditing Uses of Probabilities in Selecting and Interpreting Test Checks," *The Journal of Accountancy*, LXXXVIII (Sept., 1949), 214–217.

———, "Scientific Method in Auditing," *Accounting Research*. Cambridge, England, I (Jan., 1950), 229–234.

AUDITING STANDARDS

American Institute of Accountants, *Tentative Statements of Auditing Standards, Special Report by the Committee on Auditing Procedure*, New York, American Institute of Accountants, 1947. 43 pp.

BARNES, PARRY, "Standards of Auditing Procedure and Reports," *The Journal of Accountancy*, LXXXII (July, 1946), 45–50.

BROAD, SAMUEL J., "Auditing Standards," *The Journal of Accountancy*, LXXII (Nov., 1941), 390–397.

———, "Recent Revelopments in Accounting and Auditing," *The Journal of Accountancy*, LXXVIII (Sept., 1944), 186–193.

HAWES, HENRY C., "Auditing Standards," *The Journal of Accountancy*, LXXIV (Aug., 1942), 111–112.

JENNINGS, ALVIN R., "Standards for Field Work," in *New Developments in Accounting, 1946: Papers Presented at the Fifty-Ninth Annual Meeting of the American Institute of Accountants*. New York, The American Institute of Accountants, 1946. 206 pp.

Journal of Accountancy, "Auditing Standards" (editorial), LXXII (Nov., 1941), 385–386.

———, "Auditing Standards" (editorial), LXXIII (April, 1942), 291–292.

KRACKE, E. A., "Auditing Standards as Measures of the Auditor and His Procedures," *The Journal of Accountancy*, LXXXII (Sept., 1946), 203–210.

———, "The Personal Standards of the Auditor," in *New Developments in Accounting, 1946: Papers Presented at the Fifty-Ninth Annual Meeting of the American Institute of Accountants*. New York, The American Institute of Accountants, 1946. 206 pp.

LINDQUIST, JOHN A., "Standards of Reporting," in *New Developments in Accounting; 1946: Papers Presented at the Fifty-Ninth Annual Meeting of the American Institute of Accountants*. New York, The American Institute of Accountants, 1946. 206 pp.

RABEL, FREDERICK K., "Auditing Standards and Procedures in the Light of Court Decisions," *The Journal of Accountancy,* LXXVIII (July, 1944), 42–58.

WEBSTER, S. S., JR., "Why We Need Auditing Standards," *The Journal of Accountancy,* LXXV (May, 1943), 426–432.

RANDOM SAMPLING NUMBERS

FISHER, R. A., and F. YATES, *Statistical Tables for Biological, Agricultural and Medical Research,* London, Oliver and Boyd, 1938.

KENDALL, M. G., and B. BABINGTON SMITH, *Tables of Random Sampling Numbers. Tracts for Computers,* No. XXIV. London, Cambridge University Press, 1939.

TIPPETT, L. H. C., *Random Sampling Numbers. Tracts for Computers,* No. XV. London, Cambridge University Press, 1927.

INDEX

INDEX